THIRD EDITION

UNI 150

DESIGNING *your* MAJOR

EXPLORING *MAJORS* & *CAREERS*

ASU MAJOR & CAREER EXPLORATION

Kendall Hunt
publishing company

Cover image © ASU

Kendall Hunt
publishing company

www.kendallhunt.com
Send all inquiries to:
4050 Westmark Drive
Dubuque, IA 52004-1840

Copyright © 2016, 2017, 2018 by ASU: Major Career and Exploration

ISBN: 978-1-5249-6423-8

Published in the United States of America

CONTENTS

What Are My Interests?

Learning Objectives

Read to answer these key questions:

- What are my interests?

- What lifestyle do I prefer?

- How do my interests relate to possible careers?

Exploring Your Interests

Interests are simply what a person likes to do. As interests are developed, they can become a passion. Research shows that students who choose a major that matches their interests are more likely to earn high grades and finish their degrees.[4] It is difficult to be gritty if you are not interested in what you are doing. After college, people are more satisfied with their jobs if it matches their interests. If you like your job, both your job performance and life satisfaction increase.

How do you learn about your interests? Interests are a result of many factors, including personality, family life, values, and interaction with the environment. Part of developing an interest is trying new things and sticking with them for a while to find out if they match your interests. Participating in extracurricular activities, volunteering, internships, and working part time while in college can help you to explore your interests. One barrier to discovering your interests is unrealistic expectations. Often students are expecting the perfect job; however, every job has enjoyable aspects and aspects you don't like.

Another way to explore your interests is through vocational interest assessments. By studying people who are satisfied with their careers, psychologists have been able to help people choose careers based on their interests. The U.S. Department of Labor has developed the O*Net Interest Profiler, which helps to identify your career interests.[5] The O*Net Interest Profiler is compatible with Holland's Theory of Vocational Personality. This is one of the most widely accepted approaches to vocational choice. According to the theory, there are six vocational personality types. These six types and their accompanying definitions are presented below. As you read through each description, think about your own interests.

Realistic

People with **realistic** interests like work activities that include practical, hands-on problems and solutions. They enjoy dealing with plants, animals, and real-world materials like wood, tools, and machinery. They enjoy outside work. Often people with realistic interests do not like occupations that mainly involve doing paperwork or working closely with others.

Investigative

People with **investigative** interests like work activities that have to do with ideas and thinking more than with physical activity. They like to search for facts and figure out problems mentally rather than to persuade or lead people.

Artistic

People with **artistic** interests like work activities that deal with the artistic side of things, such as forms, designs, and patterns. They like self-expression in their work. They prefer settings where work can be done without following a clear set of rules.

Social

People with **social** interests like work activities that assist others and promote learning and personal development. They prefer to communicate more than to work with objects, machines, or data. They like to teach, give advice, help, or otherwise be of service to people.

Enterprising

People with **enterprising** interests like work activities that have to do with starting up and carrying out projects, especially business ventures. They like persuading and leading people and making decisions. They like taking risks for profit. These people prefer action rather than thought.

Conventional

People with **conventional** interests like work activities that follow set procedures and routines. They prefer working with data and detail rather than with ideas. They prefer work in which there are precise standards rather than work in which you have to judge things by yourself. These people like working where the lines of authority are clear.

According to Holland, most individuals can be described by one or more of these six personality types, frequently summarized as R-I-A-S-E-C (the first letter of each personality type). Additionally, the theory proposes that there are six corresponding work environments (or occupational groups), and that people seek out work environments that match their personality types. The better the match individuals make, the more satisfied they will be with their jobs.[6]

Holland arranged these interests on a hexagon that shows the relationship of the interests to one another. He notes that most people are not just one type, but rather a combination of types. Types that are close to each other on the hexagon are likely to have interests in common. For example, a person who is social is likely to have some artistic interests and some enterprising interests. Interests on opposite points of the hexagon are very different. For example, artistic and conventional types are opposites. Artistic types prefer freedom to be creative; conventional types prefer structure and order. The figure that follows illustrates the relationship between interest areas.[4]

> "The only way to do great work is to love what you do."
> Steve Jobs

> "Even if you're on the right track, you'll get run over if you just sit there."
> Will Rogers

> "Real success is finding your life work in work that you love."
> David McCullough

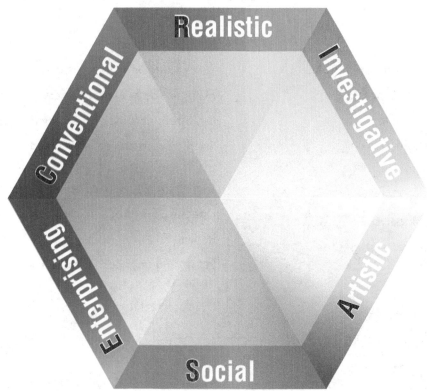

Figure 1.1 Relationships between interest areas.
© Kendall Hunt Publishing Company

The Interest Profiler[8]

Place a checkmark next to the items in each list that you might **like to do**. Keep a positive attitude when thinking about your interests. You do not need to know how to do these activities or have the opportunity to do them to select items that you might like to do in the future. Also, be careful not to select an activity just because it is likely to produce higher income. You can earn higher income by increasing your skills and education in these areas. For example, if you would like to build a brick walkway, you could work in construction, or with more education, become a civil engineer. Just indicate what you would enjoy doing. Remember that this is not a test and that there are no right or wrong answers to the questions. The goal is for you to learn more about your personal career interests and related occupations.

When you are finished with each section, tally the number of checkmarks in each area. Sample job titles for each area of interest are included. Underline any jobs that appeal to you. You can also match your interests to over 900 occupations listed at O*Net Online (https://www.onetonline.org/find/descriptor/browse/Interests/). This site includes information on specific occupations, including work tasks; tools and technology; knowledge, skills, and abilities required; work activities and work context; level of education required; work styles; work values; and wages and employment information.

Realistic (R)

I would like to:

_____ Build kitchen cabinets

_____ Guard money in an armored car

_____ Operate a dairy farm

_____ Lay brick or tile

_____ Monitor a machine on an assembly line

_____ Repair household appliances

_____ Drive a taxi cab

_____ Install flooring in houses

_____ Raise fish in a fish hatchery

_____ Build a brick walkway

_____ Assemble electronic parts

_____ Drive a truck to deliver packages to offices and homes

_____ Paint houses

_____ Enforce fish and game laws

_____ Operate a grinding machine in a factory

_____ Work on an offshore oil-drilling rig

_____ Perform lawn care services

_____ Assemble products in a factory

_____ Catch fish as a member of a fishing crew

_____ Refinish furniture

_____ Fix a broken faucet

_____ Do cleaning or maintenance work

_____ Maintain the grounds of a park

_____ Operate a machine on a production line

_____ Spray trees to prevent the spread of harmful insects

_____ Test the quality of parts before shipment

_____ Operate a motorboat to carry passengers

_____ Repair and install locks

_____ Set up and operate machines to make products

_____ Put out forest fires

R =

Matching Job Titles for Realistic Interests[9]

Construction worker, building contractor, cook, landscaper, housekeeper, janitor, firefighter, hazardous materials removal worker, security guard, truck driver, automotive mechanic, cardiovascular technologist, civil engineer, commercial pilot, computer support specialist, plumber, police officer, chemical engineer, fish and game warden, surveyor, archaeologist, athletic trainer, dentist, veterinarian

Investigative (I)

I would like to:

_____ Study space travel

_____ Make a map of the bottom of an ocean

_____ Study the history of past civilizations

_____ Study animal behavior

_____ Develop a new medicine

_____ Plan a research study

_____ Study ways to reduce water pollution

_____ Develop a new medical treatment or procedure

_____ Determine the infection rate of a new disease

_____ Study rocks and minerals

_____ Diagnose and treat sick animals

_____ Study the personalities of world leaders

_____ Conduct chemical experiments

_____ Conduct biological research

_____ Study the population growth of a city

_____ Study whales and other types of marine life

_____ Investigate crimes

_____ Study the movement of planets

_____ Examine blood samples using a microscope

_____ Investigate the cause of a fire

_____ Study the structure of the human body

_____ Develop psychological profiles of criminals

_____ Develop a way to better predict the weather

_____ Work in a biology lab

_____ Invent a replacement for sugar

_____ Study genetics

_____ Study the governments of different countries

_____ Do research on plants or animals

_____ Do laboratory tests to identify diseases

_____ Study weather conditions

I =

Matching Job Titles for Investigative Interests

Electronic engineering technician, emergency medical technician, fire investigator, paralegal, police detective, engineer (aerospace, biomedical, chemical, electrical, computer, environmental, or industrial), chemist, computer systems analyst, geoscientist, market research analyst, anesthesiologist, biochemist, biophysicist, clinical psychologist, dietician, physician, microbiologist, pharmacist, psychiatrist, surgeon, veterinarian, science teacher, college professor

Artistic (A)

I would like to:

_____ Conduct a symphony orchestra

_____ Write stories or articles for magazines

_____ Direct a play

_____ Create dance routines for a show

_____ Write books or plays

_____ Play a musical instrument

(Continued)

_____ Perform comedy routines in front of an audience

_____ Perform as an extra in movies, plays, or television shows

_____ Write reviews of books or plays

_____ Compose or arrange music

_____ Act in a movie

_____ Dance in a Broadway show

_____ Draw pictures

_____ Sing professionally

_____ Perform stunts for a movie or television show

_____ Create special effects for movies

_____ Conduct a musical choir

_____ Act in a play

_____ Paint sets for plays

_____ Audition singers and musicians for a musical show

_____ Design sets for plays

_____ Announce a radio show

_____ Write scripts for movies or television shows

_____ Write a song

_____ Perform jazz or tap dance

_____ Direct a movie

_____ Sing in a band

_____ Design artwork for magazines

_____ Edit movies

_____ Pose for a photographer

$$A =$$

Matching Job Titles for Artistic Interests

Model, actor, fine artist, floral designer, singer, tile setter, architectural drafter, architect, dancer, fashion designer, film and video editor, hairdresser, makeup artist, museum technician, music composer, photographer, self-enrichment education teacher, art director, broadcast news analyst, choreographer, editor, graphic designer, landscape architect, creative writer, public relations specialist, teacher (of art, drama, or music)

Social (S)

I would like to:

_____ Teach an individual an exercise routine

_____ Perform nursing duties in a hospital

_____ Give CPR to someone who has stopped breathing

_____ Help people with personal or emotional problems

_____ Teach children how to read

_____ Work with mentally disabled children

_____ Teach an elementary school class

_____ Give career guidance to people

_____ Supervise the activities of children at a camp

_____ Help people with family-related problems

_____ Perform rehabilitation therapy

_____ Do volunteer work at a nonprofit organization

_____ Help elderly people with their daily activities

_____ Teach children how to play sports

_____ Help disabled people improve their daily living skills

_____ Teach sign language to people with hearing disabilities

_____ Help people who have problems with drugs or alcohol

_____ Help conduct a group therapy session

_____ Help families care for ill relatives

_____ Provide massage therapy to people

_____ Plan exercises for disabled patients

_____ Counsel people who have a life-threatening illness

_____ Teach disabled people work and living skills

_____ Organize activities at a recreational facility

_____ Take care of children at a day care center

_____ Organize field trips for disabled people

_____ Assist doctors in treating patients

_____ Work with juveniles on probation

_____ Provide physical therapy to people recovering from injuries

_____ Teach a high school class

S = [   ]

Matching Job Titles for Social Interests

Host, hostess, bartender, lifeguard, food server, child care worker, home health aide, occupational therapist, occupational therapist aide, personal and home care aide, physical therapist, physical therapist aide, veterinary assistant, dental hygienist, fitness trainer, medical assistant, nanny, teacher (preschool, kindergarten, elementary, middle, or high school), registered nurse, respiratory therapist, self-enrichment education teacher, tour guide, mediator, educational administrator, health educator, park naturalist, probation officer, recreation worker, chiropractor, clergy, counseling psychologist, social worker, substance abuse counselor, physician assistant, speech and language pathologist

Enterprising (E)

I would like to:

_____ Buy and sell stocks and bonds

_____ Manage a retail store

_____ Sell telephone and other communication equipment

_____ Operate a beauty salon or barber shop

_____ Sell merchandise over the telephone

_____ Run a stand that sells newspapers and magazines

_____ Give a presentation about a product you are selling

_____ Buy and sell land

_____ Sell compact discs at a music store

_____ Run a toy store

_____ Manage the operations of a hotel

_____ Sell houses

_____ Sell candy and popcorn at sports events

_____ Manage a supermarket

_____ Manage a department within a large company

_____ Sell a soft drink product line to stores and restaurants

_____ Sell refreshments at a movie theater

_____ Sell hair-care products to stores and salons

_____ Start your own business

_____ Negotiate business contracts

_____ Represent a client in a lawsuit

_____ Negotiate contracts for professional athletes

_____ Be responsible for the operation of a company

_____ Market a new line of clothing

_____ Sell newspaper advertisements

_____ Sell merchandise at a department store

_____ Sell automobiles

_____ Manage a clothing store

_____ Sell restaurant franchises to individuals

_____ Sell computer equipment to a store

E = [   ]

(Continued)

Matching Job Titles for Enterprising Interests

Cashier, food worker, customer service representative, sales worker, supervisor, gaming dealer, inspector, retail sales clerk, chef, food service manager, operations manager, real estate broker, realtor, sheriff, wholesale or retail buyer, advertiser, appraiser, construction manager, criminal investigator, financial manager, insurance sales agent, meeting and convention planner, personal financial advisor, sales engineer, judge, lawyer, business or political science teacher, educational administrator, librarian, medical health manager, treasurer, controller

Conventional (C)

I would like to:

_____ Develop a spreadsheet using computer software

_____ Proofread records or forms

_____ Use a computer program to generate customer bills

_____ Schedule conferences for an organization

_____ Keep accounts payable/receivable for an office

_____ Load computer software into a large computer network

_____ Transfer funds between banks using a computer

_____ Organize and schedule office meetings

_____ Use a word processor to edit and format documents

_____ Operate a calculator

_____ Direct or transfer phone calls for a large organization

_____ Perform office filing tasks

_____ Compute and record statistical and other numerical data

_____ Generate the monthly payroll checks for an office

_____ Take notes during a meeting

_____ Keep shipping and receiving records

_____ Calculate the wages of employees

_____ Assist senior-level accountants in performing bookkeeping tasks

_____ Type labels for envelopes and packages

_____ Inventory supplies using a handheld computer

_____ Develop an office filing system

_____ Keep records of financial transactions for an organization

_____ Record information from customers applying for charge accounts

_____ Photocopy letters and reports

_____ Record rent payments

_____ Enter information into a database

_____ Keep inventory records

_____ Maintain employee records

_____ Stamp, sort, and distribute mail for an organization

_____ Handle customers' bank transactions

C =

Matching Job Titles for Conventional Interests

Cashier, cook, janitor, landscaping worker, resort desk clerk, medical records technician, medical secretary, bookkeeping and accounting clerk, dental assistant, drafter, loan officer, paralegal, pharmacy technician, purchasing agent, accountant, auditor, budget analyst, city and regional planner, computer security specialist, cost estimator, credit analyst, database administrator, environmental compliance inspector, financial analyst, geophysical data technician, librarian, proofreader, computer science teacher, pharmacist, statistician, treasurer

Summing Up Your Results

Put the number of checkmarks from each section of the Interest Profiler on the lines that follow:

_____ **R**ealistic   _____ **S**ocial

_____ **I**nvestigative   _____ **E**nterprising

_____ **A**rtistic   _____ **C**onventional

What are your top three areas of interest? (Realistic, Investigative, Artistic, Social, Enterprising, Conventional?)

1. _____

2. _____

3. _____

REFLECTION

List your top three areas of interest from the Interest Profiler above (realistic, investigative, social, enterprising, or conventional). Go to https://www.onetonline.org/find/descriptor/browse/Interests/ and click on your highest interests to find matching careers. List one matching career and briefly describe the education required, salary, and projected growth for the career. Here is an easy outline:

My top three interests on the Interest Profiler are . . .

One career that matches my interests is . . .

The education required is . . .

The median salary is . . .

Interests and Lifestyle

Our occupational interests determine what we study and the kinds of occupations we choose. While study and work form the basis of our lifestyle, there are other important components. What we choose to do for fun and relaxation helps us to be refreshed and keeps life interesting. Another component of a balanced lifestyle is time spent with friends and family. It is important to choose work that allows you to have the resources and time to lead a balanced lifestyle with all of these components. A balanced lifestyle has been described as a triangle with work and study forming the base, leisure and recreation forming one side, and kinship and friendship forming the other side.

Give some thought to the kind of lifestyle you prefer. Think about balancing your work, leisure, and social activities.

REFLECTION

In seeking to accomplish lifetime goals, sometimes people are not successful because they place too much emphasis on work, study, leisure, or social life. How would you balance work, study, leisure, and social life to achieve your lifetime goals?

Interests

Test what you have learned by selecting the correct answers to the following questions.

1. Realistic people are likely to choose a career in

   a. construction or engineering.
   b. accounting or real estate.
   c. financial investments or banking.

2. Investigative people are likely to choose a career in

   a. art or music.
   b. teaching or social work.
   c. science or laboratory work.

3. Enterprising people are likely to choose a career in

   a. computer programming or accounting.
   b. business management or government.
   c. health care or social services.

4. Conventional people are likely to choose a career in

   a. health care or social services.
   b. financial investments or banking.
   c. manufacturing or transportation.

5. Social types generally

   a. enjoy working with tools and machines.
   b. are humanistic and idealistic.
   c. have skills in selling and communication.

Notes

1. U.S. Department of Labor, "O*Net Interest Profiler," available at http://onetcenter.org

2. U.S. Department of Labor, "O*Net Interest Profiler User's Guide," available at http://onetcenter.org

3. John L. Holland, *Making Vocational Choices: A Theory of Vocational Personalities and Work Environments* (2nd Ed.), (Englewood Cliffs, NJ: Prentice-Hall, 1985).

4. U.S. Department of Labor, "O*Net Interest Profiler User's Guide."

5. Adapted from U.S. Department of Labor, "O*Net Interest Profiler."

6. Job titles in this section from http://www.onetonline.org/find/descriptor/browse/Interests/

How would you define the word "successful"?

Motivation Activity 2

Think about a major you've chosen or are considering and answer the following questions:

1. Why are you considering this major? What led or caused you to become interested in this choice? Why or why not?

2. Would you say that your interest in this major is motivated primarily by intrinsic factors—i.e., factors "inside" of you, such as your personal abilities, interests, needs, and values? Or is your interest in the career motivated more heavily by extrinsic factors—i.e., factors "outside" of you, such as starting salary or meeting the expectations of parents?

NOTES

What Types of Research Will Help Me Make an Informed Decision about My Major and Career?

Learning Objectives

Read to answer these key questions:

- How do I research a career?

- What are some other factors in choosing a major?

- What skills will help me successful in my career?

© Maryna Pleshkun/Shutterstock.com

Once you have completed a thorough self-assessment, you may still have several majors to consider. At this point, it is important to do some research on the outlook for a selected career in the future and the pay you would receive. Sometimes students are disappointed after graduation when they find there are few job opportunities in their chosen career field. Sometimes students graduate and cannot find jobs with the salary they had hoped to earn. It is important to think about the opportunities you will have in the future. If you have several options for a career you would enjoy, you may want to consider seriously the career that has the best outlook and pay.

According to the Bureau of Labor Statistics, fields with the best outlook include health care, computers, and the new "green jobs" related to preserving the environment. The top-paying careers all require math skills and include the science, engineering, computer science, health care, and business fields. Only 4% of college graduates choose the engineering and computer science fields. Since there are fewer students in these majors, the salaries are higher. If you have a talent or interest in math, you can develop this skill and use it in high-paying careers.

Some Majors with the Highest Earnings for Bachelor's Degrees 2017*[5]

Notice that the majors with the highest earnings require math, science, and/or business.

College Major	Beginning Median Salary	Mid-Career Median Salary
Petroleum Engineering	96,700	172,000
Actuarial Science	60,800	119,000
Chemical Engineering	69,800	119,000
Computer Science & Engineering	71,200	116,000
Nuclear Engineering	68,500	116,000
Electrical and Computer Engineering	68,100	114,000
Aeronautical Engineering	63,000	113,000
Physics & Mathematics	56,200	111,000
Government	49,600	105,000
Biomedical Engineering	62,700	104,000
Physician Assistant Studies	85,200	103,000
Finance & Real Estate	59,500	101,000
Economics	53,900	100,000

*Includes bachelor's degrees only. Excludes medicine, law, and careers requiring advanced degrees.

Other Common Majors and Earnings*[6]

Accounting and Finance	52,800	86,400
Business and Marketing	45,800	85,300
Advertising	41,400	79,800
Geology	44,800	79,800
Architecture	45,100	79,300
Biological Sciences	42,900	79,200
Fashion Design	41,400	77,700
History and Political Science	44,500	76,000
Entrepreneurship	48,000	74,600
English Literature	41,100	74,300
Foreign Languages	42,500	74,200
Business Administration	46,100	72,400
Communication	42,100	72,300
Forestry	41,500	67,400
Multimedia & Web Design	42,300	66,500
Film, Video & Media Studies	39,600	66,300
Music Performance	39,900	65,000
Criminal Justice	39,000	63,900
Art History	40,800	63,300
Hotel & Restaurant Management	50,500	62,700
Art & Design	39,500	62,600
Liberal Arts	39,100	62,300
Psychology	38,300	62,100
Secondary Education	40,200	61,400
Humanities	40,900	57,200
Elementary Education	34,700	48,900

* Includes bachelor's degrees only. Excludes medicine, law, and careers requiring advanced degrees.

Most Meaningful College Majors*[/]

Money is often not the most important consideration in choosing a major. These careers were determined to be the most meaningful with the potential for changing the world.

College Major	Beginning Salary	Mid-Career Median Salary
Medical Laboratory Science	47,900	61,500
Pastoral Ministry	32,800	36,300
Physical Therapy	60,000	86,600
Practical Nursing	45,300	58,100
Physician Assistant Studies	85,200	103,000
Diagnostic Medical Sonography	57,700	71,100
Exercise Physiology	38,400	60,300
Nursing	57,500	74,100
Respiratory Therapy	46,200	62,900
Therapeutic Recreation	35,200	47,700
Community Health Education	37,200	55,200
Dietetics	44,300	60,500
Dental Hygiene	65,400	74,900
Environmental Health & Safety	51,200	89,800
Foods and Nutrition	40,900	58,700
Health	35,700	60,700
Social Work	33,800	46,700
Child Development	32,000	42,500

*Based on an extensive survey by Payscale.com asking college graduates with a bachelor's degree, "Does your work make the world a better place to live?"

> "We act as though comfort and luxury were the chief requirements of life, when all that we need to make us really happy is something to be enthusiastic about."
> Charles Kingsley

> "Only passions, great passions, can elevate the soul to great things."
> Denis Diderot

Every career counselor can tell stories about students who ask, "What is the career that makes the most money? That's the career I want!" However, if you choose a career based on money alone, you might find it difficult and uninteresting for a lifetime of work. You might even find yourself retraining later in life for a job that you really enjoy. Remember that the first step is to figure out who you are and what you like. Then look at career outlook and opportunity. If you find your passion in a career that is in demand and pays well, you will probably be very happy with your career choice. If you find your passion in a career that offers few jobs and does not pay well, you will have to use your ingenuity to find a job and make a living. Many students happily make this informed choice and find a way to make it work.

KEYS TO SUCCESS

Mark Twain said, "The secret of success is making your vocation your vacation." Find what you like to do. Better yet, find your passion. If you can find your passion, it is easy to invest the time and effort necessary to be successful.

How do you know when you have found your passion? You have found your passion when you are doing an activity and you do not notice that the time is passing. The great painter Picasso often talked about how quickly time passed while he was painting. He said, "When I work, I relax; doing nothing or entertaining visitors makes me tired." Whether you are an artist, an athlete, a scientist, or a business entrepreneur, passion provides the energy needed to be successful. It helps you to grow and create. When you are using your talents to grow and create, you can find meaning and happiness in your life. Finding your passion can help you to be grittier too.

Psychologist Martin Seligman has written a book entitled *Authentic Happiness*, in which he writes about three types of work orientation: a job, a career, and a calling.[8] A job is what you do for the paycheck at the end of the week. Many college students have jobs to earn money for college. A career has deeper personal meaning. It involves achievement, prestige, and power. A calling is defined as "a passionate commitment to work for its own sake."[9] When you have found your calling, the job itself is the reward. He notes that people who have found their calling are consistently happier than those who have a job or even

(Continued)

a career. One of the ways that you know you have found your calling is when you are in the state of "flow." The state of "flow" is defined as "complete absorption in an activity whose challenges mesh perfectly with your abilities."[10] People who experience "flow" are happier and more productive. They do not spend their days looking forward to Friday. Understanding your personal strengths is the beginning step to finding your calling.

Seligman adds that any job can become a calling if you use your personal strengths to do the best possible job. He cited a study of hospital cleaners. Although some viewed their job as drudgery, others viewed the job as a calling. They believed that they helped patients get better by working efficiently and anticipating the needs of doctors and nurses. They rearranged furniture and decorated walls to help patients feel better. They found their calling by applying their personal talents to their jobs. As a result, their jobs became a calling.

Sometimes we wait around for passion to find us. That probably won't happen. The first step in finding your passion is to know yourself. Then find an occupation in which you can use your talents. You may be able to find your passion by looking at your present job and finding a creative way to do it based on your special talents. It has been said that there are no dead-end jobs, just people who cannot see the possibilities. Begin your search for passion by looking at your personal strengths and how you can apply them in the job market. If the job that you have now is not your passion, see what you can learn from it and then use your skills to find a career where you are more likely to find your passion.

> "Success is not the key to happiness; happiness is the key to success. If you love what you are doing, you will be successful."
> Anonymous

© Lyudmyla Kharlamova/
Shutterstock.com

College Success 1

The College Success 1 website is continually updated with supplementary material for each chapter including Word documents of the journal entries, classroom activities, handouts, videos, links to related materials, and much more. See http://www.collegesuccess1.com/.

Notes

1. Judith Provost and Scott Anchors, eds., *Applications of the Myers-Briggs Type Indicator In Higher Education* (Palo Alto, CA: Consulting Psychologists Press, 1991), 51.

2. Ibid., 49.

3. Otto Kroeger and Janet Thuesen, *Type Talk: The 16 Personality Types That Determine How We Live, Love and Work* (New York: Dell, 1989), 204.

4. Ibid.

5. Payscale, "College Salary Report 2016–17," from http://www.payscale.com/college-salary-report, accessed July 2017.

6. Ibid.

7. Ibid.

8. Martin Seligman, Authentic Happiness (Free Press, 2002).

9. Martin Seligman, as reported by Geoffrey Cowley, "The Science of Happiness," *Newsweek*, September 16, 2002, 49.

10. Ibid.

Developments Affecting Future Careers

Jobs of the future will continue to be influenced by changes in our society and economy. These new developments will affect the job market for the future:[13]

We are evolving into a service, technology, and information society. Fewer people are working in agriculture and manufacturing. Futurists note that we are moving toward a service economy based on high technology, rapid communications, biotechnology for use in agriculture and medicine, health care, and sales of merchandise.[14] Service areas with increasing numbers of jobs include health care and social assistance; professional, scientific, and technical services; education services; accommodation and food services; government; retail trade; transportation and warehousing; finance and insurance; arts, entertainment, and recreation; wholesale trade; real estate, rental, and leasing; and information management.

There will be an increased need for education. Constant change in society and innovation in technology will require lifelong learning on the job. Education will take place in a variety of forms: community college courses, training on the job, private training sessions, and learning on your own. Those who do not keep up with the new technology will find that their skills quickly become obsolete. Those who do keep up will find their skills in demand. Higher education is linked to greater earnings and increased employment opportunities.

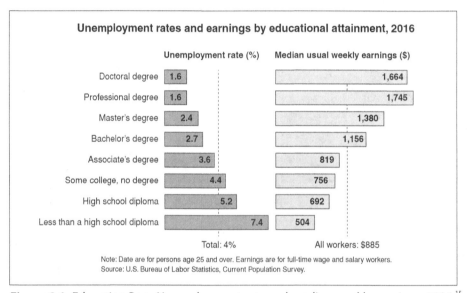

Figure 2.1 Education Pays, Unemployment rate and median weekly earnings, 2014.[15]

There will be increased opportunities for Stem (science, technology, engineering, and math) jobs. These jobs will grow 17% by 2020. These occupations jobs include many of the highest paying jobs.

Beware of job outsourcing. To reduce costs and improve profits, many jobs in technology, manufacturing, and service are being outsourced to countries such as India, China, and Taiwan, where well-educated, English-speaking workers are being used to do these jobs. For example, programmers in India can produce software at only 10% of the cost of these services in the United States. Jobs that are currently being outsources include accounting, payroll clerks, customer service, data entry, assembly line workers, industrial engineering, machine operators, computer-assisted design (CAD) technicians, purchasing managers, textile workers, software developers, and technical support. Jobs that are most likely to be outsourced are[16]

- Repetitive jobs, such as accounting,
- Well-defined jobs, such as customer service,
- Small manageable projects, such as software development,
- Jobs in which proximity to the customer is not important, such as technical support.

Jobs that are least likely to be outsourced include

- Jobs with ambiguity, such as top management jobs,
- Unpredictable jobs, such as troubleshooters,
- Jobs that require understanding of the culture, such as marketing,
- Joss that require close proximity to the customer, such as auto repair,
- Jobs requiring a high degree of innovation and creativity, such as product design,
- Jobs in entertainment, music, art, and design.

To protect yourself from outsourcing,

- Strive to be the best in the field.
- Be creative and innovative.
- Avoid repetitive jobs that do not require proximity to the customer.
- Choose a career where the demand is so high that it won't matter if some are outsourced.
- Consider a job in the skilled trades: carpenters, plumbers, electricians, hair stylists, construction workers, auto mechanics, and dental hygienists will always be in demand.

Globalization is changing the job market. Multinational corporations will locate their companies based on the availability of workers and the cost of labor. This trend will reduce the cost of goods and services but will change the nature of the job market. While this trend has resulted in outsourcing, there are increasing numbers of jobs in the United States requiring workers who speak different languages and understand how to do business in other countries.

Nontraditional jobs are increasing. Unlike traditional workers, nontraditional workers do not have full-time, year-round jobs with health and retirement benefits. Employers are moving toward using nontraditional workers, including multiple job holders, contingent and part-time workers, independent contractors, and temporary workers. Nearly four out of five employers use nontraditional workers to help them become more efficient, prevent layoffs, and access workers with special skills. There are advantages and disadvantages to this arrangement. Nontraditional workers have no benefits and risk unemployment. However, this arrangement can provide workers with a flexible work schedule in which they work during some periods and pursue other interests or gain new skills when not working.

© Mathias Rosenthal/Shutterstock.com

Automation will continue to reduce repetitive jobs in every industry. Increasingly sophisticated robots will be used to decrease the cost of goods and services. Engineers and technicians will be needed to design and maintain these robots.

There is a mismatch between workers and available jobs. It is often difficult for companies to fill jobs requiring highly skilled technical and scientific workers. These workers are often hired in other countries and use technology to work remotely.

More companies will use teleworking. Teleworking involves using smart phones to do some work at home. Currently, about 40% of workers use their smart phones to do some work at home. As a result, there will be increased flexibility of work hours and more people will work remotely using smart devices. There will be increased demand for application designers and designers for smart devices.

E-commerce is changing the way we do business. E-commerce is the purchasing of goods, services, and information over the Internet. More people are using e-commerce because of convenience, selection, cost savings, and ease of shopping. Online sales are a growing part of the market, increasing 10–20% a year for the past several years. By 2017, the web will account for 10% of retail sales, and approximately 43% of sales are influenced by online research.[17] There are more career opportunities in related fields such as computer graphics, web design, online marketing, and package delivery services.

Business will increase virtual collaboration. Workers are increasingly using Skype and other collaboration software to work with others.

New media literacy will become an essential skill for most new jobs. Workers who do not keep up with new media will quickly find their skills obsolete.

Career Trends for 2020

The good news is that over 20 million new jobs will be created by 2020, which represents a 14% annual growth rate. Approximately 60% of the competitive, high-demand, and high-paying jobs will require at least a bachelor's degree. Majors most in demand include accounting, engineering, computer science, business, and economics. However, most college students are majoring in history, education, and social science, which are lower in demand. Here are some specific areas where there will be increasing demand in the future.[18]

Data analysis. Companies are increasingly using data for market research. Opportunities exist for those who can find and analyze data.

Mental health. After being neglected for a long time, people are beginning to understand the importance of mental health for safety and the enjoyment of life. Current health-care insurance includes mental health coverage that will result in increased demand for services.

Technology-related jobs will continue to increase. Information and technology workers are now the largest group of workers in the United States. The Bureau of Labor Statistics reports that two million technology-related jobs will be created by 2018. Jobs in computer systems design and related services are expected to increase by 34% by 2018.[19]

Careers in **information technology** include the design, development, and support of computers, software, hardware, and networks. Some newer jobs in this area include animation for video games, film, videos, setting up websites, and Internet security. Jobs that will grow faster than the average include computer network administrators, data communications analysts, web developers, and App designers. Some new fields include data loss prevention, online security, and risk management. Computer science degrees are especially marketable when combined with traditional majors such as finance, accounting, or marketing. [20]

Radiation and laser technologies will provide new technical careers in the future. It has been said that lasers will be as important to the 21st century as electricity was for the 20th century. New uses for lasers are being found in medicine, energy, industry, computers, communications, entertainment, and outer space. The use of lasers is creating new jobs and causing others to become obsolete. For example, many welders are being replaced by laser technicians, who have significantly higher earnings. New jobs will open for people who purchase, install, and maintain lasers.

Careers in fiber optics and telecommunications are among the top new emerging fields in the 21st century. Fiber optics are thin glass fibers that transmit light. This new technology may soon make copper wire obsolete. One of the most important uses of fiber optics is to speed up delivery of data over the Internet and to improve telecommunications. It is also widely used in medical instruments, including laser surgery.

Artificial intelligence has interesting possibilities for the future. It enables computers to recognize patterns, improve from experience, make inferences, and approximate human thought. Artificial intelligence will be increasingly used in robots and smart machines. Two recent examples are IPhone's Siri, which uses voice recognition software to search the Internet, and Google's development of the self-driving car.

Research. There will be high demand for people with advanced degrees in engineering, chemistry, math, biology, biotechnology, and other sciences who will be the innovators in technology, medicine, and manufacturing.

Biology. Future historians may describe the 21st century as the biology century because of all the developments in this area. One of the most important developments is the Human Genome Project, which has identified the genes in human DNA, the carrier of genetic material. This research has resulted in new careers in biotechnology and biomedical technology.

Biotechnology will become increasingly important as a way to combat disease, develop new surgical procedures and devices, increase food production, reduce pollution, improve recycling, and provide new tools for law enforcement. Biotechnology includes genomic profiling, biomedical engineering, new pharmaceuticals, genetic engineering, and DNA identification. In the future, biotechnology may be used to find cures for diabetes, arthritis, Alzheimer's disease, and heart disease.

The field of **biomedical engineering,** which involves developing and testing healthcare innovations, is expected to grow by 72% by 2018.[21] Biomedical technology is the field in which bionic implants are being developed for the human body. Scientists are working on the development of artificial limbs and organs including eyes, ears, hearts, and kidneys. A promising new development in this field is brain and computer interfaces. Scientists recently implanted a computer chip into the brain of a quadriplegic, enabling him to control a computer and television with his mind.[22] Biotechnology also develops new diagnostic test equipment and surgical tools.

Veterinary medicine. The demand for veterinarians is expected to increase by 35% because of the demand for pet products and health. However, it is interesting to note that there will be 35 times as many jobs for nurses as for veterinarians.[23]

Health-care occupations will add the most new jobs between 2012 and 2022 and registered nurses will see the most job growth.[24] This trend is being driven by an aging

© zhang kan/Shutterstock.com

population, increased longevity, health-care reform, and new developments in the pharmaceutical and medical fields. Demand will be especially high for dentists, nurses, physician specialists, optometrists, physical therapists, audiologists, pharmacists, athletic trainers, and elder-care providers. Because of increasing health-care costs, many of the jobs done by doctors, nurses, dentists, or physical therapists are now being done by physician's assistants, dental assistants, physical therapy aides, and home health aides. Health-care workers will increasingly use technology to do their work. For example, a new occupation is nursing informatics, which combines traditional nursing skills with computer and information science. Health care will be continually connected to technology such as in the biomedical engineering field.

Environmental science. There will be increased demand for limited resources requiring new technology to conserve water, control pollution, manage global warming, and produce food.

Green jobs are occupations dealing with the efficient use of energy, finding renewable sources of energy, and preserving the environment. As fossil fuels are depleted, the world is facing a major transformation in how energy is generated and used. Sustainability, wind turbines, solar panels, farmer's markets, biofuels, and wind energy are just some of the ways to transition to a post-fossil fuel world. Jobs in this field include engineers who design new technology, consultants to audit energy needs, and technicians who install and maintain systems. Here are some titles of green jobs: environmental lawyer, environmental technician, sustainability consultant, sustainability project director, green architect, green building project manager, marine biologist, environmental technician, energy efficiency specialist, organic farmer, compliance manager, product engineer, wind energy engineer, and solar engineer.

Finance. Money management has become increasingly complex and important requiring professionals who understand finance, investments, and taxes.

Business. Today's business managers need to understand increased competition, the global economy, and must stay up-to-date with the latest forms of communication and social media. The median salaries in this category range from 70,000 to 80,000 and beyond making this occupation a good choice for those interested in higher incomes. Jobs with fast growth include market research analysts, marketing specialists, personal financial advisers, and health-care managers.

Entrepreneurship and small business. An important trend for the new millennium is the increase in entrepreneurship, which means starting your own business. Small

© Kheng Guan Toh/Shutterstock.com

businesses that can find innovative ways of meeting customer needs will be in demand for the future. A growing number of entrepreneurs operate their small businesses from home, taking advantage of telecommuting and the Internet to communicate with customers. While being an entrepreneur has some risks involved, there are many benefits, such as flexible scheduling, being your own boss, taking charge of your destiny, and greater potential for future income if your company is successful. You won't have to worry about being outsourced either.

Teaching. As the current generation of Baby Boomers retires, there will be increased jobs for educators who will serve the children of the New Millennial generation.

The effect of terrorism and the need for security. Fear of terrorism has changed attitudes that will affect career trends for years to come. Terrorist attacks have created an atmosphere of uncertainty that has had a negative effect on the economy and has increased unemployment. People are choosing to stay in the safety of their homes, offices, cars, and gated communities. Since people are spending more time at home, they spend more money making their homes comfortable. As a result, construction, home remodeling, and sales of entertainment systems are increasing.

Another result of terrorism is the shift toward occupations that provide value to society and in which people can search for personal satisfaction. More people volunteer their time to help others and are considering careers in education, social work, and medical occupations. When people are forced to relocate because of unemployment, they are considering moving to smaller towns that have a sense of community and a feeling of safety.

As the world population continues to grow, there is continued conflict over resources and ideologies and an increased need for security and safety. Law enforcement, intelligence, forensics, international relations, foreign affairs, and security administration careers will be in demand.

Careers with a Good Outlook for the Future

Jobs That Will Always Be in Demand[25]	2016 Best Jobs Rankings[26]	Top 10 Jobs for the Next Decade and Beyond[27]
Teachers	App Developer	Computer Programmer
Lawyers	Nurse Practitioner	Day Care Provider
Engineers	Information Security Analyst	Elder Care Specialist
Doctors	Computer Systems Analyst	Employment Specialist
Law Enforcement	Physical Therapist	Environmental Engineer
Accountants	Market Research Analyst	Home Health Aide
Food Preparers and Servers	Medical Sonographer	Management Consultant
	Dental Hygienist	Networking Specialist
	Operations Research Analyst	Physician's Assistant
	Health Services Manager	Social Services Coordinator

REFLECTION

Do a quick review of the developments affecting future careers and career trends for 2020. Write one paragraph about how any of these trends might affect your future.

Top Jobs for the Future[28]

Based on current career trends, here are some jobs that should be in high demand for the next 10 years.

Field of Employment	Job Titles
Business	Marketing Manager, Security and Financial Service, Internet Marketing Specialist, Advertising Executive, Buyer, Sales Person, Real Estate Agent, Business Development Manager, Marketing Researcher, Recruiter
Education	Teacher, Teacher's Aide, Adult Education Instructor, Math and Science Teacher
Entertainment	Dancer, Producer, Director, Actor, Content Creator, Musician, Artist, Commercial Artist, Writer, Technical Writer, Newspaper Reporter, News Anchor Person
Health	Emergency Medical Technician, Surgeon, Chiropractor, Dental Hygienist, Registered Nurse, Medical Assistant, Therapist, Respiratory Therapist, Home Health Aide, Primary Care Physician, Medical Lab Technician, Radiology Technician, Physical Therapist, Dental Assistant, Nurse's Aide
Information Technology	Computer Systems Analyst, Computer Engineer, Web Specialist, Network Support Technician, Java Programmer, Information Technology Manager, Web Developer, Database Administrator, Network Engineer
Law/Law Enforcement	Correction Officer, Law Officer, Anti-Terrorist Specialist, Security Guard, Tax/Estate Attorney, Intellectual Property Attorney
Services	Veterinarian, Social Worker, Hair Stylist, Telephone Repair Technician, Aircraft Mechanic, Guidance Counselor, Occupational Therapist, Child Care Assistant, Baker, Landscape Architect, Pest Controller, Chef, Caterer, Food Server
Sports	Athlete, Coach, Umpire, Physical Trainer
Technology	Electrical Engineer, Biological Scientist, Electronic Technician, CAD Operator, Product Designer, Sales Engineer, Applications Engineer, Product Marketing Engineer, Technical Support Manager, Product Development Manager
Trades	Carpenter, Plumber, Electrician
Travel/Transportation	Package Delivery Person, Flight Attendant, Hotel/Restaurant Manager, Taxi Driver, Chauffeur, Driver

QUIZ

Career Trends of the Future

Test what you have learned by selecting the correct answers to the following questions:

1. Students in Generation Z are

    a. limited by technology.
    b. more likely to have a lifetime career.
    c. more likely to appreciate ethnic diversity.

2. Use of the Internet will result in

    a. increased e-commerce.
    b. increased use of conventional stores.
    c. decreased mail delivery.

3. The largest group of workers in the United States is in

    a. manufacturing.
    b. information technology.
    c. agriculture.

4. Jobs unlikely to be outsourced include

    a. jobs that require close proximity to the customer.
    b. computer programming jobs.
    c. customer service jobs.

5. Future historians will describe the 21st century as the

    a. art and entertainment century.
    b. biology century.
    c. industrial development century.

Work Skills for the 21st Century

Because of rapid changes in technology, college students of today may be preparing for jobs that do not exist right now. After graduation, many college students find employment that is not even related to their college majors. One researcher found that 48 percent of college graduates find employment in fields not related to their college majors.[29] More important than one's college major are the general skills learned in college that prepare students for the future.

To define skills needed in the future workplace, the U.S. Secretary of Labor created the Secretary's Commission on Achieving Necessary Skills (SCANS). Based on interviews with employers and educators, the members of the commission outlined foundation skills and workplace competencies needed to succeed in the workplace in the 21st century.[30] The following skills apply to all occupations in all fields and will help you to become a successful employee, regardless of your major. As you read through these skills, think about your competency in these areas.

Foundation Skills

Basic Skills

- Reading
- Writing
- Basic arithmetic
- Higher-level mathematics
- Listening
- Speaking

© iQoncept/Shutterstock.com

Thinking Skills

- Creative thinking
- Decision making
- Problem solving
- Mental visualization
- Knowing how to learn
- Reasoning

Personal Qualities

- Responsibility
- Self-esteem
- Sociability
- Self-management
- Integrity/honesty

© VLADGRIN/Shutterstock.com

Workplace Competencies

The following are some workplace competencies required to be successful in all well-paying jobs. The successful employee:

- can manage resources such as time, money, materials, and human resources;
- has good interpersonal skills and can participate as a member of a team, teach others, serve clients and customers, exercise leadership, negotiate workable solutions, and work with diverse individuals;
- can learn new information on the job and use computers to acquire, organize, analyze, and communicate information;
- works within the system, monitors and corrects performance, and improves the system as needed;
- uses technology to produce the desired results.

Because the workplace is changing, these skills may be more important than the background acquired through a college major. Work to develop these skills and you will be prepared for whatever lies ahead.

How to Research Your Career

After you have assessed your personality, interests, values, and talents, the next step is to learn about the world of work. If you can match your personal strengths to the world of work, you can find work that is interesting and you can excel in it. To learn about the world of work, you will need to research possible careers. This includes reading career descriptions and investigating career outlooks, salaries, and educational requirements.

Career Descriptions

The career description tells you about the nature of the work, working conditions, employment, training, qualifications, advancement, job outlook, earnings, and related occupations. The two best sources of job descriptions are the *Occupational Outlook Handbook* and *Occupational Outlook Quarterly*. The *Handbook*, published by the Bureau of Labor Statistics, is like an encyclopedia of careers. You can search alphabetically by career or by career cluster.

The *Occupational Outlook Quarterly* is a periodical with up-to-date articles on new and emerging occupations, training opportunities, salary trends, and new studies from the Bureau of Labor Statistics. You can find these resources in a public or school library, at a college career center, or on the *College Success Website* at http://www.collegesuccess1.com/Links9Career.htm.

Career Outlook

It is especially important to know about the career outlook of an occupation you are considering. Career outlook includes salary and availability of employment. How much does the occupation pay? Will the occupation exist in the future, and will there be employment opportunities? Of course, you will want to prepare yourself for careers that pay well and have future employment opportunities.

You can find information about career outlooks in the sources listed above, current periodicals, and materials from the Bureau of Labor Statistics. The following table, for example, lists the fastest-growing occupations, occupations with the highest salaries, and occupations with the largest job growth. Information from the Bureau of Labor Statistics is also available online.

> "The supreme accomplishment is to blur the line between work and play."
> Arnold Toynbee

> "Starting out to make money is the greatest mistake in life. Do what you feel you have a flair for doing, and if you are good enough at it, the money will come."
> Greer Garson

© iQoncept/Shutterstock.com

Employment Projections 2008–2018[31]

10 Fastest-Growing Occupations	10 Industries with the Largest Wage and Salary Employment Growth	10 Occupations with the Largest Numerical Job Growth
Biomedical engineers	Management, scientific, technical	Registered nurses
Network systems and data communications analysts	Physicians	Home health aides
Home health aides	Computer systems design and related	Customer service representatives
Personal and home care aides	General merchandise stores	Food preparation workers
Financial examiners	Employment services	Personal and home care aides
Medical scientists	Local government	Retail salespersons
Physician assistants	Home health care services	Office clerks
Skin care specialists	Services for elderly and disabled	Accountants and auditors
Biochemists and biophysicists	Nursing care facilities	Nursing aides, orderlies
Athletic trainers	Full-service restaurants	Postsecondary teachers

Exercise 1. Work Values

Name _____   Occupation #2_____

Work values are qualities about a job that are most significant and meaningful to you. Without them, the job would not be satisfying. Identify ten work values that are important to you and rank them from 1 to 10, 1 being most important.

_____ Great salary
_____ Recognition from others
_____ Security
_____ Fun
_____ Autonomy
_____ Variety
_____ Excitement
_____ Lots of leisure time
_____ Leadership role
_____ Helping others
_____ Prestige
_____ Creativity
_____ Improving society
_____ Influencing others
_____ Continuity
_____ Professional position

_____ Flexible work schedule
_____ Working outside
_____ Having an office
_____ Congenial workplace
_____ Competition
_____ Travel
_____ Affiliation
_____ Decision making
_____ Supervising others
_____ Work flexibility
_____ Public contact
_____ Working alone
Other
_____ a. _____
_____ b. _____
_____ c. _____

1. What are your top three work values?

2. Describe why each of these values is important to you.

What Are the Benefits of an Informational Interview?

Learning Objectives

Read to answer these key questions:

- What is an informational interview?

- What are some employment trends for the future?

- What are work skills necessary for success in the twenty-first century?

Informational Interviewing

The informational interview is an informal conversation useful for finding career information, exploring your career, building your network, or possibly finding future employment. It is not a job interview and the purpose is not to find employment. It is a way to find more personal information about a career you may be considering and to see if you are a good fit for this occupation.

The informational interview differs from the traditional interview in that you are in control and can ask questions about daily job tasks and how they relate to your interests. It is a great way to build your self-confidence and prepare you for an actual job interview. To obtain an informational interview, check your LinkedIn contacts to see if anyone you know is employed in the industry. Ask your friends, family, and employers if they can recommend someone for the interview. You can also work with your college Career Services to see if they have contacts for informational interviews. They often have contacts with college alumni who are willing to speak with students. You can visit websites to identify individuals you would like to interview. Most professionals enjoy helping others who have an interest in their field.

Regard the informational interview as a business appointment and dress the way others dress in this occupation. Make a short appointment (generally 15–30 minutes), state that the purpose of the appointment is to gain career information and advice, and show up on time. You can suggest that the person meet you for coffee (and be sure to pay the bill yourself). Be prepared with a list of questions to ask and to take some brief notes on the information. To begin the interview, give a brief 30 second overview of your career goals and reasons for contacting this person. Remember that the focus of the interview is to find career information. It is best not to ask for a job at this time. If there is a job available and you are a good fit for the job, he or she will likely tell you about it.

It is important to thank the interviewee and then follow up a thank you note or email. Ask the person if he or she is on LinkedIn and if you can request a link online. Bring your resume and hand it to the person at the end of the interview. Do not begin the interview with the resume since you want the focus on career information rather than on yourself.

Here is a sample phone call asking for an informational interview:

Hello. My name is _____ and I am a student at _____University. I found your name at your company website. (Or _____ gave me your name and suggested that I contact you.) Although I am not currently looking for a job, I am interested in the field of _____ and would like to learn more about this occupation. Would it be possible to schedule 15–30 minutes of your time to ask a few questions and get your advice on how to enter this field?

© 2013, Shutterstock, Inc.

Following is a list of potential interview questions that you can use to keep the conversation going. You probably won't have time to ask all these questions, so choose the ones most that are most personally relevant.

1. What is your job title? What other job titles are commonly used for this position?

2. How did you get this position? What was your career path from entry-level to the position you now have?

3. What are your key job responsibilities? What is the typical day like for you?

4. What skills and education are needed for this job?

5. What are the most valuable courses that you took to prepare you for this job?

6. What are employers looking for (skills, education, personal qualities)?

7. What certificates or degrees are required for this job?

8. What kinds of internships or work experiences are desirable? Are internships available?

9. How does a person obtain this type of employment? How is the job advertised? Is the job market competitive? How can I meet the competition?

10. What are some entry-level positions in this company?

11. What important words should I include on my resume or cover letter?

12. What are the opportunities for advancement?

13. What are some personal characteristics that lead to success on this job?

14. What do you find most satisfying about your job?

15. What are the best and worst things about working in this job? What do you like about your job? Dislike?

16. What stresses you out about your job? What is the most difficult part of your job?

17. What are some of the most important challenges facing your industry today? How will it change in the next 10 years?

18. What is the salary range? What is the potential for advancement?

19. If you were still a college student, what would it be helpful to know about your current job and how to find employment in your field?

20. Can you suggest other sources or persons who could be valuable sources of information for me?

It is always easier to get where you are going if you have a road map or a plan. To start the journey, it is helpful to know about yourself, including your personality, interests, talents, and values. Once you have this picture, you will need to know about the world of work and job trends that will affect your future employment opportunities. Next, you will need to make decisions about which road to follow. Then, you will need to plan your education to reach your destination. Finally, you will need some job-seeking skills such a writing a resume and cover letter, using social media to market yourself online, and preparing for a successful interview.

© Kiselev Andrey Valerevich/Shutterstock.com

Keep Your Eyes on the Future

The world is changing quickly, and these changes will affect your future career. To assure your future career success, you will need to become aware of career trends and observe how they change over time so that you can adjust your career plans accordingly. For example, recently a school was established for training bank tellers. The school quickly went out of business and the students demanded their money back because they were not able to get jobs. A careful observer of career trends would have noticed that bank tellers are being replaced by automatic teller machines (ATMs) and would not have started a school for training bank tellers. Students observant of career trends would not have paid money for the training. It is probably a good idea for bank tellers to look ahead and plan a new career direction.

How can you find out about career trends that may affect you in the future? Become a careful observer by reading about current events. Good sources of information include:

- Your local newspaper, especially the business section
- News programs
- Current magazines
- Government statistics and publications
- The Internet

When thinking about future trends, use your critical thinking skills. Sometimes trends change quickly or interact in different ways. For example, since we are using email to a great extent today, it might seem that mail carriers would not be as much in demand in the future. However, since people are buying more goods over the Internet, there has been an increased demand for mail carriers and other delivery services. Develop the habit of looking at what is happening to see if you can identify trends that may affect your future.

Usually trends get started as a way to meet the following needs:[1]

- To save money
- To reduce cost
- To do things faster
- To make things easier to use
- To improve safety and reliability
- To lessen the impact on the environment

The following are some trends to watch that may affect your future career. As you read about each trend, think about how it could affect you.

Baby Boomers, Generation X, the Millennials and the New Generation Z

About every 20 years, sociologists begin to describe a new generation with similar characteristics based on shared historical experiences. Each generation has different opportunities and challenges in the workplace.

The Baby Boomers were born following World War II between 1946 and 1964. Four out of every 10 adults today are in this Baby Boom Generation.[2] Because there are so many aging Baby Boomers, the average age of Americans is increasing. Life expectancy is also increasing. In 2016 the projected life expectancy is 76.3 for men and 81.2 for women.[3] In the new millennium, many more people will live to be 100 years old or more! Think about the implications of an older population. Older people need such things as health care, recreation, travel, and financial planning. Occupations related to these needs are likely to be in demand now and in the future.

Those born between 1965 and 1977 are often referred to as Generation X. They are sometimes called the "baby bust" generation because fewer babies were born during this period than in the previous generations. There is much in the media about this generation having to pay higher taxes and Social Security payments to support the large number of aging Baby Boomers. Some say that this generation will not enjoy the prosperity of the Baby Boomers. Those who left college in the early nineties faced a recession and the worst job market since World War II.[4] Many left college in debt and returned home to live with their parents. Because of a lack of employment opportunities, many in this generation became entrepreneurs, starting new companies at a faster rate than previous generations.

Jane Bryant Quinn notes that in spite of economic challenges, Generation Xers have a lot going for them:[5]

- They have record-high levels of education, which correlate with higher income and lower unemployment.
- Generation Xers are computer literate, and those who use computers on the job earn 10 to 15 percent more than those who don't.
- This group often has a good work ethic valued by employers. However, they value a balanced lifestyle with time for outside interests and family.
- As Baby Boomers retire, more job opportunities are created for this group.
- Unlike the Baby Boomers, this generation was born into a more integrated and more diverse society. They are better able than previous generations to adapt to diversity in society and the workplace.

Those in the New Millennial Generation were born between 1977 and 1995. This generation is sometimes called Generation Y or the Echo Boomers, since they are the children of the Baby Boomers.[6] This new generation of approximately 60 million is three times larger than Generation X and will eventually exceed the number of Baby Boomers.

Millennials are more ethnically diverse than previous generations with 34 percent ethnic minorities. One in four lives with a single parent; three in four have working mothers. Most of them started using computers before they were five years old. Marketing researchers describe this new generation as "technologically adept, info-savvy, a cybergeneration, the clickeratti."[7] They are the connected generation, accustomed to cell phones, chatting on the Internet, and listening to downloaded music.

Young people in the Millennial Generation share a different historical perspective from the Baby Boom Generation. Baby Boomers remember the Vietnam War and the assassinations of President John F. Kennedy and Martin Luther King. For Millennials, school shootings such as Columbine and acts of terrorism such as the Oklahoma City bombing and the 9–11 attack on New York City stand out as important events. The Millennial Generation will see their main problems as dealing with violence, easy access to weapons, and the threat of terrorism.

Neil Howe and William Strauss paint a very positive picture of this new generation in their book *Millennials Rising: The Next Great Generation*:

- Millennials will rebel by tearing down old institutions that do not work and building new and better institutions. The authors predict that this will be the can-do generation filled with technology planners, community shapers, institution builders, and world leaders.
- Surveys show that this generation describes themselves as happy, confident, and positive.
- They are cooperative team players.
- They generally accept authority and respect their parents' values.
- They follow rules. The rates of homicides, violent crime, abortion, and teen pregnancy are decreasing rapidly.
- The use of alcohol, drugs, and tobacco is decreasing.
- Millennials have a fascination with and mastery of new technology.
- Their most important values are individuality and uniqueness.[8]

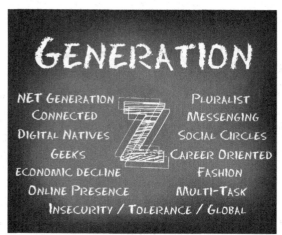

© Vaju Ariel/Shutterstock.com

In the past, new generations emerged about every twenty years. However, because of rapid social change, generations are now being defined in shorter time periods. **A new generation born since 1995 is currently emerging.** Various names for this generation have been proposed such as Generation Z, Generation Wii, the iGeneration, Gen Tech, Digital Natives, Net Gen, and the Plurals.[9] These names reflect this generation's fascination and ease of using technology as well as their increasing diversity. This is a large generation with one in four Americans under 18 years old.[10]

This generation has been affected by historical events such as the election of President Obama (the first biracial president), events surrounding 9/11, wars in Iraq and Afghanistan, the tsunami and nuclear meltdown in Japan, school violence, and economic recession. They are referred to as digital natives since they have always lived in a world with the Internet, smart phones, and other devices.

Some characteristic of this new generation include:[11]

- This is the last generation with a Caucasian majority. Only 55% of this generation is Caucasian as compared to 72% of Baby Boomers. In 2019, less than 50% of births will be Caucasian.

- They are more positive than older Americans about becoming an ethnically diverse society and more likely to have friends from different racial, ethnic, and religious groups.

- There is a continuing decline in two-parent households with only two out of three people from two parent households. Increased same sex marriage is changing the definition of family.

- Women are more likely to get a college degree and hold 51% of managerial and professional jobs. As a result, gender roles are blending with men assuming more familial responsibilities.

- It is an age of "girl power." Girls ages 8–15 care more about their grades than boys and have more expectations of receiving a college degree and having work that changes the world.

- Technology will continue to influence this group as in the New Millennial Generation. Use of technology will transform the way that people communicate and purchase goods. People will communicate with shorter and more immediate communications such as texting and Twitter. More purchases will be made on the Internet.

- This generation hopes to use technology as a tool to change the world.

It is predicted that the world of work for both the Millennials and Generation Z will be dramatically different. Previous generations anticipated having a lifetime career. By the year 2020, many jobs will probably be short-term contracts. This arrangement will provide cost savings and efficiency for employers and flexibility for employees to start or stop work to take vacations, train for new jobs, or meet family responsibilities. One in five people will be self-employed. Retirement will be postponed as people look forward to living longer and healthier lives.[12]

REFLECTION

Describe your generation (Baby Boomer, Generation X, New Millennial or Generation Z.) What are your best qualities and challenges?

Assignment - Career Research

Name _____   Occupation #1_____

Please thoroughly complete each question using information from online resources discussed in class. For each question, please state three pieces of information.

Do not copy word-for-word from ANY source, please put it in your own words to avoid plagiarism concerns

1. Nature of Work (What you do):

2. Working Conditions (Where and how you do the work):

3. Educational and Certification Requirements:

4. Employment and Job Outlook (Are people needed NOW in this field)/ Earnings, Salary Range:

5. ASU majors that will prepare you for this career:

6. Classes offered at ASU that could give you a "taste" for this career path:

7. Contact information for someone currently working in this field: (E-mail, phone number)

8. Sources of Additional Information (websites, books, referral sources):

9. Identify, explain and describe how this occupation matches your interests? List specific examples of interests and hobbies that you have.

10. Given that a career is not likely to fit all of our interests and fulfill all of our needs, what are your interests and needs that would not be met by this career? Explain your answer. (None is not an accepointsable answer.)

11. How did you first hear about this career? What were the sources of your information (e.g., TV, movies, magazines, someone you knew, etc.? How accurate do you think are these information and portrayals?

Name _____   Occupation #2_____

Please thoroughly complete each question. For each question, please state three pieces of information.

Do not copy word-for-word from ANY source, please put it in your own words to avoid plagiarism concerns

1. Nature of Work (What you do):

2. Working Conditions (Where and how you do the work):

3. Educational and Certification Requirements:

4. Employment and Job Outlook (Are people needed NOW in this field)/ Earnings, Salary Range:

5. ASU majors that will prepare you for this career:

6. Classes offered at ASU that could give you a "taste" for this career path:

7. Contact information for someone currently working in this field: (E-mail, phone number)

8. Sources of Additional Information (websites, books, referral sources):

9. Identify, explain and describe how this occupation matches your interests? List specific examples of interests and hobbies that you have.

10. Given that a career is not likely to fit all of our interests and fulfill all of our needs, what are your interests and needs that would not be met by this career? Explain your answer. (None is not an accepointsable answer.)

11. How did you first hear about this career? What were the sources of your information (e.g., TV, movies, magazines, someone you knew, etc.? How accurate do you think are these information and portrayals?

Assignment - Career Research Summary

	Limited / Not Addressed	Adequate	Excellent
Responses to questions 1-8 completed	Nothing present. (0 points)	Minimal and/or incomplete information for each question. (2 points)	All aspects of questions are completed. (4.5 points)
Reflection Questions 9-11	Topics briefly addressed without explanation. Some component of question not present. Nothing present. (0 points)	Bare minimum responses. One component is not addressed. No deeper explanation or reflection. (2 points)	Thoughtful and introspective responses. Analysis skill (why and how) utilized. Paper demonstrates synthesis and integration. (4.5 points)
Overall Assignment Writing	Numerous spelling and grammar mistakes. Incomplete sentences. (0 points)	Some incomplete sentences and frequent spelling and grammar errors. (.5 points)	No spelling or grammatical errors. Complete sentences. (1 point)
Total Points (5 points per occupation)			

Why Is Diversity Important in the Workplace?

Learning Objectives

Read to answer these key questions:

- What is diversity and why is it important?

- How can an understanding and appreciation of diversity help me to be successful in school and in work?

- What is some vocabulary useful for understanding diversity?

- What are some ideas for communicating across cultures?

- How can I gain an appreciation of diversity?

- What are strategies for overcoming stereotyping and prejudice?

Diversity

Learning about and from Human Differences

Chapter Preview

Learning Goal

Ignite Your Thinking

This chapter clarifies what "diversity" really means and demonstrates how experiencing diversity can deepen learning, promote critical and creative thinking, and contribute to your personal and professional development. Strategies are provided for overcoming cultural barriers and biases that block the development of rewarding relationships with diverse people and learning from others whose cultural backgrounds differ from our own. Simply stated, we learn more from people that are different from us than we do from people similar to us. There's more diversity among college students today than at any other time in history. This chapter will help you capitalize on this learning opportunity.

Gain greater appreciation of human differences and develop skills for making the most of diversity in college and beyond.

REFLECTION

Complete the following sentence:
When I hear the word *diversity*, the first thing that comes to my mind is . . .

What Is Diversity?

Literally translated, the word "diversity" derives from the Latin root *diversus*, meaning "various" or "variety." Thus, human diversity refers to the variety that exists in humanity (the human species). The relationship between humanity and diversity may be compared to the relationship between sunlight and the variety of colors that make up the visual spectrum. Similar to how sunlight passing through a prism disperses into the variety of colors that comprise the visual spectrum, the human species on planet earth is dispersed into a variety of different groups that comprise the human spectrum (humanity). Figure 4.1 illustrates this metaphorical relationship between diversity and humanity.

As depicted in the above figure, human diversity is manifested in a multiplicity of ways, including differences in physical features, national origins, cultural backgrounds, and sexual orientations. Some dimensions of diversity are easily detectable, others are very subtle, and some are invisible.

REFLECTION

Look at the diversity spectrum in Figure 4.1 and look over the list of groups that make up the spectrum. Do you notice any groups missing from the list that should be added, either because they have distinctive backgrounds or because they've been targets of prejudice and discrimination?

SPECTRUM
of
DIVERSITY

Gender (male-female)
Age (stage of life)
Race (e.g., White, Black, Asian)
Ethnicity (e.g., Native American, Hispanic, Irish, German)
Socioeconomic status (job status/income)
National *citizenship* (citizen of U.S. or another country)
Native (first-learned) *language*
National *origin* (nation of birth)
National *region* (e.g., raised in north/south)
Generation (historical period when people are born and live)
Political ideology (e.g., liberal/conservative)
Religious/spiritual beliefs (e.g., Christian/Buddhist/Muslim)
Family status (e.g., single-parent/two-parent family)
Marital status (single/married)
Parental status (with/without children)
Sexual orientation (heterosexual/homosexual/bisexual)
Physical ability/disability (e.g., able to hear/deaf)
Mental ability/disability (e.g., mentally able/challenged)
Learning ability/disability (e.g., absence/presence of dyslexia)
Mental health/illness (e.g., absence/presence of depression)

HUMANITY →

_ _ _ _ _ _ _ = dimension of diversity

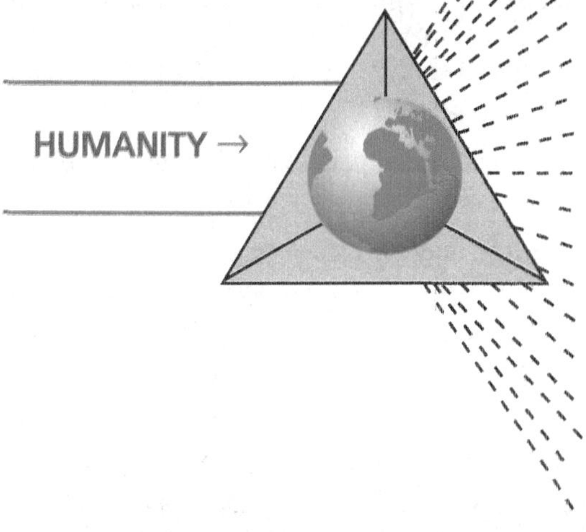

*This list represents some of the major dimensions of human diversity; it does not constitute a complete list of all possible forms of human diversity. Also, disagreement exists about certain dimensions of diversity (e.g., whether certain groups should be considered races or ethnic groups).

©Kendall Hunt Publishing Company

Figure 4.1 Humanity and Diversity

Diversity includes discussion of equal rights and social justice for minority groups, but it's a broader concept that involves much more than political issues. In a national survey of American voters, the vast majority of respondents agreed that diversity is more than just "political correctness" (National Survey of Women Voters, 1998). Diversity is also an *educational* issue—an integral element of a college education that contributes to the learning, personal development, and career preparation of *all* students. It enhances the quality of the college experience by bringing multiple perspectives and alternative approaches to *what* is being learned (the content) and *how* it's being learned (the process).

> Ethnic and cultural diversity is an integral, natural, and normal component of educational experiences for all students."
> —National Council for Social Studies

Note

Diversity is a human issue that embraces and benefits all people; it's not a code word for "some" people. Although one major goal of diversity is to promote appreciation and equitable treatment of particular groups of people who've experienced discrimination, it's also a learning experience that strengthens the quality of a college education, career preparation, and leadership potential.

What Is Racial Diversity?

A *racial group (race)* is a group of people who share distinctive physical traits, such as skin color or facial characteristics. The variation in skin color we now see among humans is largely due to biological adaptations that have evolved over thousands of years among groups of humans who migrated to different climatic regions of the world. Currently, the most widely accepted explanation of the geographic origin of modern humans is the "Out of Africa" theory. Genetic studies and fossil evidence indicate that all Homo sapiens inhabited Africa 150,000–250,000 years ago; over time, some migrated from Africa to other parts of the world (Mendez, et al., 2013; Meredith, 2011; Reid & Hetherington, 2010). Darker skin tones developed among humans who inhabited and reproduced in hotter geographical regions nearer the equator (e.g., Africans). Their darker skin color helped them adapt and survive by providing them with better protection from the potentially damaging effects of intense sunlight (Bridgeman, 2003). In contrast, lighter skin tones developed over time among humans inhabiting colder climates that were farther from the equator (e.g., Scandinavia). Their lighter skin color enabled them to absorb greater amounts of vitamin D supplied by sunlight, which was in shorter supply in those regions of the world (Jablonksi & Chaplin, 2002).

Currently, the U.S. Census Bureau has identified five races (U.S. Census Bureau, 2013b):

White: a person whose lineage may be traced to the original people inhabiting Europe, the Middle East, or North Africa.

Black or African American: a person whose lineage may be traced to the original people inhabiting Africa.

American Indian or Alaska Native: a person whose lineage may be traced to the original people inhabiting North and South America (including Central America), and who continue to maintain their tribal affiliation or attachment.

Asian: a person whose lineage may be traced to the original people inhabiting the Far East, Southeast Asia, or the Indian subcontinent, including: Cambodia, China, India, Japan, Korea, Malaysia, Pakistan, the Philippine Islands, Thailand, and Vietnam.

Native Hawaiian or Other Pacific Islander: a person whose lineage may be traced to the original people inhabiting Hawaii, Guam, Samoa, or other Pacific islands.

It's important to keep in mind that racial categories are not based on scientific evidence; they merely represent group classifications constructed by society (Anderson & Fienberg, 2000). No identifiable set of genes distinguishes one race from another; in fact, there continues to be disagreement among scholars about what groups of people constitute a human race or whether distinctive races actually exist (Wheelright, 2005). In other words, you can't do a blood test or some type of internal genetic test to determine a person's race. Humans have simply decided to categorize themselves into races on the basis of certain external differences in their physical appearance, particularly the color of their outer layer of skin. The U.S. Census Bureau could have decided to divide people into "racial" categories based on other physical characteristics, such as eye color (blue, brown, and green), hair color (brown, black, blonde, or red), or body length (tall, short, or mid-sized).

AUTHOR'S EXPERIENCE

My father stood approximately six feet tall and had straight, light brown hair. His skin color was that of a Western European with a very slight suntan. My mother was from Alabama; she was dark in skin color with high cheekbones and had long curly black hair. In fact, if you didn't know that my father was of African American descent, you would not have thought he was black.

All of my life I've thought of myself as African American and all people who know me have thought of me as African American. I've lived half of a century with that as my racial identity. Several years ago, I carefully reviewed records of births and deaths in my family history and discovered that I had less than 50% African lineage. Biologically, I am no longer black; socially and emotionally, I still am. Clearly, my "race" has been socially constructed, not biologically determined.

—Aaron Thompson

While humans may display diversity in the color or tone of their external layer of skin, the reality is that all members of the human species are remarkably similar at an internal biological level. More than 98% of the genes of all humans are exactly the same, regardless of what their particular race may be (Bronfenbrenner, 2005). This large amount of genetic overlap accounts for our distinctively "human" appearance, which clearly distinguishes us from all other living species. All humans have internal organs that are similar in structure and function, and despite variations in the color of our outer layer of skin, when it's cut, all humans bleed in the same color.

AUTHOR'S EXPERIENCE

I was sitting in a coffee shop in the Chicago O'Hare airport while proofreading my first draft of this chapter. I looked up from my work for a second and saw what appeared to be a white girl about 18 years of age. As I lowered my head to return to work, I did a double-take and looked at her again because something about her seemed different or unusual. When I looked more closely at her the second time, I noticed that although she had white skin, the features of her face and hair appeared to be those of an African American. After a couple of seconds of puzzlement, I figured it out: she was an *albino* African American. That satisfied my curiosity for the moment, but then I began to wonder: Would it still be accurate to say she was "black" even though her skin was not black? Would her hair and facial features be sufficient for her to be considered or classified as black? If yes, then what would be the "race" of someone who had black skin tone, but did not have the typical hair and facial features characteristic of black people? Is skin color the defining feature of being African American or are other features equally important?

I was unable to answer these questions, but found it amusing that all of these thoughts were crossing my mind while I was working on a chapter dealing with diversity. On the plane ride home, I thought again about that albino African American girl and realized that she was a perfect example of how classifying people into "races" isn't based on objective, scientific evidence, but on subjective, socially constructed categories.

—*Joe Cuseo*

Categorizing people into distinct racial or ethnic groups is becoming even more difficult because members of different ethnic and racial groups are increasingly forming cross-ethnic and interracial families. By 2050, the number of Americans who identify themselves as being of two or more races is projected to more than triple, growing from 7.5 million to 26.7 million (U.S. Census Bureau, 2013a).

REFLECTION

What race(s) do you consider yourself to be?

Would you say you identify strongly with your racial identity, or are you rarely conscious of it? Why?

What Is Cultural Diversity?

"Culture" may be defined as a distinctive pattern of beliefs and values learned by a group of people who share the same social heritage and traditions. In short, culture is the whole way in which a group of people has learned to live (Peoples & Bailey, 2011); it includes their style of speaking (language), fashion, food, art and music, as well as their beliefs and values. Box 4.1 contains a summary of key components of culture that a group may share.

REFLECTION

Look at the components of culture cited in the previous list. Add another aspect of culture to the list that you think is important or influential. Explain why you think this is an important element of culture.

Box 4.1

Key Components of Culture

Language: How members of the culture communicate through written or spoken words; their particular dialect; and their distinctive style of nonverbal communication (body language).

Space: How cultural members arrange themselves with respect to social–spatial distance (e.g., how closely they stand next to each other when having a conversation).

Time: How the culture conceives of, divides, and uses time (e.g., the speed or pace at which they conduct business).

Aesthetics: How cultural members appreciate and express artistic beauty and creativity (e.g., their style of visual art, culinary art, music, theater, literature, and dance).

Family: The culture's attitudes and habits with respect to interacting with family members (e.g., customary styles of parenting their children and caring for their elderly).

Economics: How the culture meets its members' material needs, and its customary ways of acquiring and distributing wealth (e.g., general level of wealth and gap between the very rich and very poor).

Gender Roles: The culture's expectations for "appropriate" male and female behavior (e.g., whether or not women are able to hold the same leadership positions as men).

Politics: How decision-making power is exercised in the culture (e.g., democratically or autocratically).

Science and Technology: The culture's attitude toward and use of science or technology (e.g., the degree to which the culture is technologically "advanced").

Philosophy: The culture's ideas or views on wisdom, goodness, truth, and social values (e.g., whether they place greater value on individual competition or collective collaboration).

Spirituality and Religion: Cultural beliefs about a supreme being and an afterlife (e.g., its predominant faith-based views and belief systems about the supernatural).

I was watching a basketball game between the Los Angeles Lakers and Los Angeles Clippers when a short scuffle broke out between the Lakers' Paul Gasol—who is Spanish—and the Clippers' Chris Paul—who is African American. After the scuffle ended, Gasol tried to show Paul there were no hard feelings by patting him on the head. Instead of interpreting Gasol's head pat as a peace-making gesture, Paul took it as a putdown and returned the favor by slapping (rather than patting) Paul in the head.

This whole misunderstanding stemmed from a basic difference in nonverbal communication between the two cultures. Patting someone on the head in European cultures is a friendly gesture; European soccer players often do it to an opposing player to express no ill will after a foul or collision. However, this same nonverbal message meant something very different to Chris Paul—an African American raised in urban America.

—Joe Cuseo

What Is an Ethnic Group?

A group of people who share the same culture is referred to as an *ethnic group*. Thus, "culture" refers to *what* an ethnic group shares in common (e.g., language and traditions) and "ethnic group" refers to the *people* who share the same culture that's been *learned* through common social experiences. Members of the same racial group—whose shared physical characteristics have been *inherited*—may be members of different ethnic groups. For instance, white Americans belong to the same racial group, but differ in terms of their ethnic group (e.g., French, German, Irish) and Asian Americans belong to the same racial group, but are members of different ethnic groups (e.g., Japanese, Chinese, Korean).

Currently, the major cultural (ethnic) groups in the United States include:

- Native Americans (American Indians)
  - Cherokee, Navaho, Hopi, Alaskan natives, Blackfoot, etc.
- European Americans (Whites)
  - Descendents from Western Europe (e.g., United Kingdom, Ireland, Netherlands), Eastern Europe (e.g., Hungary, Romania, Bulgaria), Southern Europe (e.g., Italy, Greece, Portugal), and Northern Europe or Scandinavia (e.g., Denmark, Sweden, Norway)
- African Americans (Blacks)
  - Americans whose cultural roots lie in the continent of Africa (e.g., Ethiopia, Kenya, Nigeria) and the Caribbean Islands (e.g., Bahamas, Cuba, Jamaica)
- Hispanic Americans (Latinos)
  - Americans with cultural roots in Mexico, Puerto Rico, Central America (e.g., El Salvador, Guatemala, Nicaragua), and South America (e.g., Brazil, Columbia, Venezuela)
- Asian Americans
  - Americans whose cultural roots lie in East Asia (e.g., Japan, China, Korea), Southeast Asia (e.g., Vietnam, Thailand, Cambodia), and South Asia (e.g., India, Pakistan, Bangladesh)
- Middle Eastern Americans
  - Americans with cultural roots in Iraq, Iran, Israel, etc.

Culture is a distinctive pattern of beliefs and values that develops among a group of people who share the same social heritage and traditions.

REFLECTION

What ethnic group(s) are you a member of, or do you identify with? What would you say are the key cultural values shared by your ethnic group(s)?

European Americans are still the majority ethnic group in the United States; they account for more than 50% of the American population. Native Americans, African Americans, Hispanic Americans, and Asian Americans are considered to be *minority* ethnic groups because each of these groups represents less than 50% of the American population (U.S. Census Bureau, 2015).

As with racial grouping, classifying humans into different ethnic groups can be very arbitrary and subject to debate. Currently, the U.S. Census Bureau classifies Hispanics as an ethnic group rather than a race. However, among Americans who checked "some other race" in the 2000 Census, 97% were Hispanic. This finding suggests that Hispanic Americans consider themselves to be a racial group, probably because that's how they're perceived and treated by non-Hispanics (Cianciatto, 2005). It's noteworthy that the American media used the term "racial profiling" (rather than ethnic profiling) to describe Arizona's controversial 2010 law that allowed police to target Hispanics who "look" like illegal aliens from Mexico, Central America, and South America. Once again, this illustrates how race and ethnicity are subjective, socially constructed concepts that reflect how people perceive and treat different social groups, which, in turn, affects how members of these groups perceive themselves.

I'm the only person from my race in class."
—Hispanic student commenting on why he felt uncomfortable in his class on race, ethnicity, and gender

The Relationship between Diversity and Humanity

As previously noted, diversity represents variations on the same theme: being human. Thus, humanity and diversity are interdependent, complementary concepts. To understand human diversity is to understand both our differences and *similarities*. Diversity appreciation includes appreciating both the unique perspectives of different cultural groups as well as universal aspects of the human experience that are common to all groups—whatever their particular cultural background happens to be. Members of all racial and ethnic groups live in communities, develop personal relationships, have emotional needs, and undergo life experiences that affect their self-esteem and personal identity. Humans of all races and ethnicities experience similar emotions and reveal those emotions with similar facial expressions (see Figure 4.2).

Other characteristics that anthropologists have found to be shared by all humans in every corner of the world include: storytelling, poetry, adornment of the body, dance, music, decoration with artifacts, families, socialization of children by elders, a sense of right and wrong, supernatural beliefs, and mourning of the dead (Pinker, 2000). Although different cultural groups may express these shared experiences in different ways, they are universal experiences common to all human cultures.

REFLECTION

In addition to those already mentioned, can you think of another important human experience that is universal—that is experienced by all humans?

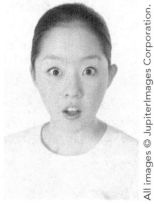

All images © JupiterImages Corporation.

Figure 4.2

You may have heard the question: "We're all human, aren't we?" The answer to this important question is "yes and no." Yes, we are all the same, but not in the same way. A good metaphor for understanding this apparent contradiction is to visualize humanity as a quilt in which we're all united by the common thread of humanity—the universal bond of being human (much like the quilt below). The different patches comprising the quilt represent diversity—the distinctive or unique cultures that comprise our shared humanity. The quilt metaphor acknowledges the identity and beauty of all cultures. It differs from the old American "melting pot" metaphor, which viewed cultural differences as something to be melted down and eliminated. It also differs from the old "salad bowl" metaphor that depicted America as a hodgepodge or mishmash of cultures thrown together without any common connection. In contrast, the quilt metaphor suggests that the unique cultures of different human groups should be preserved, recognized, and valued; at the same time, these cultural differences join together to form a seamless, unified whole. This blending of diversity and unity is captured in the Latin expression *E pluribus unum* ("Out of many, one")—the motto of the United States—which you'll find printed on all its currency.

© steven r. hendricks/Shutterstock.com

Note

When we appreciate diversity in the context of humanity, we capitalize on the variety and versatility of human differences while preserving the collective strength and synergy of human unity.

AUTHOR'S EXPERIENCE

When I was 12 years old and living in New York City, I returned from school one Friday and my mother asked me if anything interesting happened at school that day. I told her that the teacher went around the room asking students what they had for dinner the night before. At that moment, my mother became a bit concerned and nervously asked me: "What did you tell the teacher?" I said: "I told her and the rest of the class that I had pasta last night because my family always eats pasta on Thursdays and Sundays." My mother exploded and fired back the following question at me in a very agitated tone, "Why didn't you tell her we had steak or roast beef?" For a moment, I was stunned and couldn't figure out what I'd done wrong or why I should have lied about eating pasta. Then it dawned on me: My mom was embarrassed about being Italian American. She wanted me to hide our family's ethnic background and make it sound like we were very "American."

As I grew older, I understood why my mother felt the way she did. She grew up in America's "melting pot" generation—a time when different American ethnic groups were expected to melt down and melt away their ethnicity. They were not to celebrate their diversity; they were to eliminate it.

—Joe Cuseo

What Is Individuality?

It's important to keep in mind that there are individual differences among members of any racial or ethnic group that are greater than the average difference between groups. Said in another way, there's more variability (individuality) within groups than between groups. For example, among members of the same racial group, individual differences in their physical attributes (e.g., height and weight) and psychological characteristics (e.g., temperament and personality) are greater than any average difference that may exist between their racial group and other racial groups (Caplan & Caplan, 2008).

Note

While it's valuable to learn about differences between different human groups, there are substantial individual differences among people within the same racial or ethnic group that should neither be ignored nor overlooked. Don't assume that individuals with the same racial or ethnic characteristics share the same personal characteristics.

As you proceed through your college experience, keep the following key distinctions in mind:

- Humanity. All humans are members of the *same group*—the human species.
- Diversity. All humans are members of *different groups*—such as, different racial and ethnic groups.
- Individuality. Each human is a *unique individual* who differs from all other members of any group to which he or she may belong.

> I realize that I'm black, but I like to be viewed as a person, and this is everybody's wish."
> —Michael Jordan, Hall of Fame basketball player

> Every human is, at the same time, like all other humans, like some humans, and like no other human."
> —Clyde Kluckholn, American anthropologist

Major Forms or Types of Diversity in Today's World

Ethnic and Racial Diversity

America is rapidly becoming a more racially and ethnically diverse nation. Minorities now account for almost 37% of the total population—an all-time high; in 2011, for the first time in U.S. history, racial and ethnic minorities made up more than half (50.4%) of all children born in America (Nhan, 2012). By the middle of the 21st century, minority groups are expected to comprise 57% of the American population and more than 60% of the nation's children will be members of minority groups (U.S. Census Bureau, 2015).

More specifically, by 2050 the American population is projected to be more than 29% Hispanic (up from 15% in 2008), 15% Black (up from 13% in 2008), 9.6% Asian (up from 5.3% in 2008), and 2% Native Americans (up from 1.6% in 2008). The Native Hawaiian and Pacific Islander population is expected to more than double between 2008 and 2050. During this same timeframe, the percentage of white Americans will decline from 66% (2008) to 46% (2050). As a result of these demographic trends, today's ethnic and racial minorities will become the "new majority" of Americans by the middle of the 21st century (U.S. Census Bureau, 2015) (see Figure 4.3).

The growing racial and ethnic diversity of America's population is reflected in the growing diversity of students enrolled in its colleges and universities. In 1960, whites made up almost 95% of the total college population; in 2010, that percentage had decreased to 61.5%. Between 1976 and 2010, the percentage of ethnic minority students in higher education increased from 17% to 40% (National Center for Education Statistics, 2011). This rise in ethnic and racial diversity on American campuses is particularly noteworthy when viewed in light of the historical treatment of minority groups in the United States. In the early 19th century, education was not a right, but a privilege available only to those

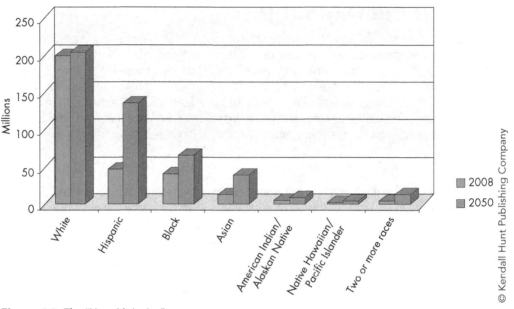

Figure 4.3 The "New Majority"

who could afford to attend private schools, which was experienced largely by Protestants of European descent (Luhman, 2007).

REFLECTION

1. What diverse groups do you see represented on your campus?

2. Are there groups on campus you didn't expect to see or to see in such large numbers?

3. Are there groups on campus you expected to see but don't see or, see in smaller numbers than you expected?

> Being born in the elite in the U.S. gives you a constellation of privileges that very few people in the world have ever experienced. Being born poor in the U.S. gives you disadvantages unlike anything in Western Europe, Japan and Canada."
>
> —David I. Levine, economist and social mobility researcher

Socioeconomic Diversity

Human diversity also exists among groups of people in terms of their socioeconomic status (SES), which is determined by their level of education, level of income, and the occupational prestige of the jobs they hold. Groups are stratified (divided) into lower, middle, or upper classes, and groups occupying lower social strata have less economic resources and social privileges (Feagin & Feagin, 2007).

Young adults from high-income families are more than seven times likely to have earned a college degree and hold a prestigious job than those from low-income families (Olson, 2007). Sharp discrepancies also exist in income level among different racial, ethnic, and gender groups. In 2012, the median income for non-Hispanic white households was $57,009, compared to $39,005 for Hispanics and $33,321 for African Americans (DeNavas-Walt, Proctor, & Smith, 2013). From 2005 to 2009, household wealth fell by 66% for Hispanics, 53% for blacks, and 16% for whites, largely due to the housing and mortgage collapse—which had a more damaging effect on lower-income families (Kochlar, Fry, & Taylor, 2011).

Despite its overall wealth, the United States is one of the most impoverished of all developed countries in the world (Shah, 2008). The poverty rate in the United States is almost twice the rate of other economically developed countries around the world (Gould & Wething, 2013). In 2012, more than 16% of the American population, and almost 20% of American children, lived below the poverty line ($23,050 yearly income for a family of four) (U.S. Census Bureau, 2013b).

REFLECTION

What do you think is the factor that's most responsible for poverty in:

a) the United States?

b) the world?

International Diversity

If it were possible to reduce the world's population to a village of precisely 100 people, with all existing human ratios remaining about the same, the demographics of this world village would look something like this:

61 would be Asians; 13 would be Africans; 12 would be Europeans; 9 would be Latin Americans; and 5 would be North Americans (citizens of the United States and Canada)
50 would be male, 50 would be female
75 would be non-white; 25 white
67 would be non-Christian; 33 would be Christian
80 would live in substandard housing
16 would be unable to read or write
50 would be malnourished and 1 would be dying of starvation
33 would be without access to a safe water supply
39 would lack access to modern sanitation
24 would have no electricity (and of the 76 who have electricity, most would only use it for light at night)
8 people would have access to the Internet
1 would have a college education
1 would have HIV
2 would be near birth; 1 near death
5 would control 32% of the entire world's wealth; all 5 would be U.S. citizens
48 would live on less than $2 a day
20 would live on less than $1 a day (Family Care Foundation, 2015).

In this world village, English would not be the most common language spoken; it would be third, following Chinese and Spanish (Lewis, Paul, & Fennig, 2014).

The need for American college students to develop an appreciation of international diversity is highlighted by a study conducted by an anthropologist who went "undercover" to pose as a student in a university residence hall. She found that the biggest complaint international students had about American students was their lack of knowledge of other countries and the misconceptions they held about people from different nations (Nathan, 2005). When you take the time to learn about other countries and the cultures of people who inhabit them, you move beyond being just a citizen of your own nation, you become *cosmopolitan*—a citizen of the world.

Generational Diversity

Humans are also diverse with respect to the historical time period in which they grew up. The term "generation" refers to a cohort (group) of individuals born during the same period in history whose attitudes, values, and habits have been shaped by events that took place in the world during their formative years of development. People growing up in different generations are likely to develop different attitudes and beliefs because of the different historical events they experienced during their upbringing.

Box 4.2 contains a brief summary of different generations, the key historical events they experienced, and the personal characteristics commonly associated with each generational group (Lancaster, Stillman, & Williams, 2002).

Box 4.2

Generational Diversity: A Snapshot Summary

- The Traditional Generation (a.k.a. "Silent Generation") (born 1922–1945). This generation was influenced by events such as the Great Depression and World Wars I and II. Characteristics associated with people growing up at this time include loyalty, patriotism, respect for authority, and conservatism.

- The Baby Boomer Generation (born 1946–1964). This generation was influenced by events such as the Vietnam War, Watergate, and the civil rights movement. Characteristics associated with people growing up at this time include idealism, emphasis on self-fulfillment, and concern for social justice and equal rights.

- Generation X (born 1965–1980). This generation was influenced by Sesame Street, the creation of MTV, AIDS, and soaring divorce rates. They were the first "latchkey children"—youngsters who used their own key to let themselves into their home after school—because their mother (or single mother) was working outside the home. Characteristics associated with people growing up at this time include self-reliance, resourcefulness, and ability to adapt to change.

- Generation Y (a.k.a. "Millennials") (born 1981–2002). This generation was influenced by the September 11, 2001, terrorist attack on the United States, the shooting of students at Columbine High School, and the collapse of the Enron Corporation. Characteristics associated with people growing up at this time include a preference for working and playing in groups, familiarity with technology, and willingness to engage in volunteer service in their community (the "civic generation"). This is also the most ethnically diverse generation, which may explain why they're

more open to diversity than previous generations and are more likely to view diversity positively.

> You guys [in the media] have to get used to it. This is a new day and age, and for my generation that's a very common word. It's like saying 'bro.' That's how we address our friends. That's how we talk."
> —Matt Barnes, 33-year-old, biracial professional basketball player, explaining to reporters after being fined for using the word "niggas" in a tweet to some of his African American teammates

- Generation Z (a.k.a. "The iGeneration") (born 1994–present). This generation includes the latter half of Generation Y. They grew up during the wars in Afghanistan and Iraq, terrorism, the global recession and climate change. Consequently, they have less trust in political systems and industrial corporations than previous generations. During their formative years, the world wide web was in place, so they're quite comfortable with technology and rely heavily on the Internet, Wikipedia, Google, Twitter, MySpace, Facebook, Instant Messaging, image boards, and YouTube. They expect immediate gratification through technology and accept the lack of privacy associated with social networking. For these reasons, they're also referred to as the "digital generation."

Look back at the characteristics associated with your generation. Which of these characteristics accurately reflect your personal characteristics and those of your closest friends? Which do not?

Sexual Diversity: Gay, Lesbian, Bisexual, and Transgender (GLBT)

Humans experience and express sexuality in diverse ways. "Sexual diversity" refers to differences in human *sexual orientation*—the gender (male or female) an individual is physically attracted to, and *sexual identity*—the gender an individual identifies with or considers himself or herself or to be. The spectrum of sexual diversity includes:

Heterosexuals—males who are sexually attracted to females, and females who are sexually attracted to males

Gays—males who are sexually attracted to males

Lesbians—females who are sexually attracted to females

Bisexuals—individuals who are sexually attracted to males and females

Transgender—individuals who do not identify with the gender they were assigned at birth, or don't feel they belong to a single gender (e.g., transsexuals, transvestites, and bigender)

College campuses across the country are increasing their support for GLBT (gay, lesbian, bisexual, transgendered) students, creating centers and services to facilitate their acceptance and adjustment. These centers and services play an important role in combating homophobia and related forms of sexual prejudice on campus, while promoting awareness and tolerance of all forms of sexual diversity. By accepting individuals who span the spectrum of sexual diversity, we acknowledge and appreciate the reality that heterosexuality isn't the one-and-only form of human sexual expression (Dessel, Woodford, Warren, 2012). This growing acknowledgment is reflected in the Supreme Court's historic decision to legalize same-sex marriage nationwide (Dolan & Romney, 2015).

The Benefits of Experiencing Diversity

Thus far, this chapter has focused on *what* diversity is; we now turn to *why* diversity is worth experiencing. National surveys show that by the end of their first year in college, almost two-thirds of students report "stronger" or "much stronger" knowledge of people from different races and cultures than they had when they first began college, and the majority of them became more open to diverse cultures, viewpoints and values (HERI, 2013; HERI, 2014). Students who develop more openness to and knowledge of diversity are likely to experience the following benefits.

It is difficult to see the picture when you are inside the frame."
—An old saying (author unknown)

Diversity Increases Self-Awareness and Self-Knowledge

Interacting with people from diverse backgrounds increases self-knowledge and self-awareness by enabling you to compare your life experiences with others whose experiences may differ sharply from your own. When you step outside yourself to contrast your experiences with others from different backgrounds, you move beyond ethnocentrism and gain a *comparative perspective*—a reference point that positions you to see how your particular cultural background has shaped the person you are today.

A comparative perspective also enables us to learn how our cultural background has advantaged or disadvantaged us. For instance, learning about cross-cultural differences in education makes us aware of the limited opportunities people in other countries have to attend college and how advantaged we are in America—where a college education is available to everyone, regardless of their race, gender, age, or prior academic history.

Note
The more you learn from people who are different than yourself, the more you learn about yourself.

Diversity Deepens Learning

Research consistently shows that we learn more from people who differ from us than we do from people similar to us (Pascarella, 2001; Pascarella & Terenzini, 2005). Learning about different cultures and interacting with people from diverse cultural groups provides our brain with more varied routes or pathways through which to connect (learn) new ideas. Experiencing diversity "stretches" the brain beyond its normal "comfort zone," requiring it to work harder to assimilate something unfamiliar. When we encounter the unfamiliar, the brain has to engage in extra effort to understand it by comparing and contrasting it to something we already know (Acredolo & O'Connor, 1991; Nagda, Gurin, & Johnson, 2005). This added expenditure of mental energy results in the brain forming neurological connections that are deeper and more durable (Willis, 2006). Simply stated, humans learn more from diversity than they do from similarity or familiarity. In contrast, when we restrict the diversity of people with whom we interact (out of habit or prejudice), we limit the breadth and depth of our learning.

> "When the only tool you have is a hammer, you tend to see every problem as a nail."
>
> —Abraham Maslow, humanistic psychologist, best known for his self-actualization theory of human motivation

Diversity Promotes Critical Thinking

Studies show that students who experience high levels of exposure to various forms of diversity while in college—such as participating in multicultural courses and campus events and interacting with peers from different ethnic backgrounds—report the greatest gains in:

- thinking *complexly*—ability to think about all parts and sides of an issue (Association of American Colleges & Universities, 2004; Gurin, 1999),
- *reflective* thinking—ability to think deeply about personal and global issues (Kitchener, Wood, & Jensen, 2000), and
- *critical* thinking—ability to evaluate the validity of their own reasoning and the reasoning of others (Gorski, 2009; Pascarella, et al., 2001).

These findings are likely explained by the fact that when we're exposed to perspectives that differ from our own, we experience "cognitive dissonance"—a state of cognitive (mental) disequilibrium or imbalance that "forces" our mind to consider multiple perspectives simultaneously; this makes our thinking less simplistic, more complex, and more comprehensive (Brookfield, 1987; Gorski, 2009).

> "What I look for in musicians is generosity. There is so much to learn from each other and about each other's culture. Great creativity begins with tolerance."
>
> —Yo-Yo Ma, French-born, Chinese-American virtuoso cellist, composer, and winner of multiple Grammy Awards

Diversity Stimulates Creative Thinking

Cross-cultural knowledge and experiences enhance personal creativity (Leung, et al., 2008; Maddux & Galinsky, 2009). When we have diverse perspectives at our disposal, we have more opportunities to shift perspectives and discover "multiple partial solutions" to problems (Kelly, 1994). Furthermore, ideas acquired from diverse people and cultures can "cross-fertilize," giving birth to new ideas for tackling old problems (Harris, 2010). Research shows that when ideas are generated freely and exchanged openly in groups comprised of people from diverse backgrounds, powerful "cross-stimulation" effects can occur, whereby ideas from one group member trigger new ideas among other group members (Brown, Dane, & Durham, 1998). Research also indicates that seeking out diverse alternatives, perspectives, and viewpoints enhances our ability to reach personal goals (Stoltz, 2014).

Note

By drawing on ideas generated by people from diverse backgrounds and bouncing your ideas off them, divergent or expansive thinking is stimulated; this leads to synergy (multiplication of ideas) and serendipity (unexpected discoveries).

In contrast, when different cultural perspectives are neither sought nor valued, the variety of lenses available to us for viewing problems is reduced, which, in turn, reduces our capacity to think creatively. Ideas are less likely to diverge (go in different directions); instead, they're more likely to converge and merge into the same cultural channel—the one shared by the homogeneous group of people doing the thinking.

Diversity Enhances Career Preparation and Career Success

Whatever line of work you decide to pursue, you're likely to find yourself working with employers, coworkers, customers, and clients from diverse cultural backgrounds. America's workforce is now more diverse than at any other time in history and will grow ever more diverse throughout the 21st century; by 2050, the proportion of American workers from minority ethnic and racial groups will jump to 55% (U.S. Census Bureau, 2008).

National surveys reveal that policymakers, business leaders, and employers seek college graduates who are more than just "aware" of or "tolerant" of diversity. They want graduates who have actual *experience* with diversity (Education Commission of the States, 1995) and are able to collaborate with diverse coworkers, clients, and customers (Association of American Colleges & Universities, 2002; Hart Research Associates, 2013). Over 90% of employers agree that all students should have experiences in college that teach them how to solve problems with people whose views differ from their own (Hart Research Associates, 2013).

The current "global economy" also requires skills relating to international diversity. Today's work world is characterized by economic interdependence among nations, international trading (imports/exports), multinational corporations, international travel, and almost instantaneous worldwide communication—due to rapid advances in the world wide web (Dryden & Vos, 1999; Friedman, 2005). Even smaller companies and corporations have become increasingly international in nature (Brooks, 2009). As a result, employers in all sectors of the economy now seek job candidates who possess the following skills and attributes: sensitivity to human differences, ability to understand and relate to people from different cultural backgrounds, international knowledge, and ability to communicate in a second language (Fixman, 1990; National Association of Colleges & Employers, 2014; Office of Research, 1994; Hart Research Associates, 2013).

As a result of these domestic and international trends, *intercultural competence* has become an essential skill for success in the 21st century (Thompson & Cuseo, 2014). Intercultural competence may be defined as the ability to appreciate and learn from human differences and to interact effectively with people from diverse cultural backgrounds. It includes "knowledge of cultures and cultural practices (one's own and others), complex cognitive skills for decision making in intercultural contexts, social skills to function effectively in diverse groups, and personal attributes that include flexibility and openness to new ideas" (Wabash National Study of Liberal Arts Education, 2007).

When all men think alike, no one thinks very much."
—Walter Lippmann, distinguished journalist and originator of the term "stereotype"

The benefits that accrue to college students who are exposed to racial and ethnic diversity during their education carry over in the work environment. The improved ability to think critically, to understand issues from different points of view, and to collaborate harmoniously with co-workers from a range of cultural backgrounds all enhance a graduate's ability to contribute to his or her company's growth and productivity."
—Business/Higher Education Forum

Technology and advanced communications have transformed the world into a global community, with business colleagues and competitors as likely to live in India as in Indianapolis. In this environment, people need a deeper understanding of the thinking, motivations, and actions of different cultures, countries and regions."
—The Partnership for 21st Century Skills

What intercultural skills do you think you already possess?

What intercultural skills do you think you need to develop?

Note

The wealth of diversity on college campuses today represents an unprecedented educational opportunity. You may never again be a member of a community with so many people from such a wide variety of backgrounds. Seize this opportunity to strengthen your education and career preparation.

Overcoming Barriers to Diversity

Before we can capitalize on the benefits of diversity, we need to overcome obstacles that have long impeded our ability to appreciate and seek out diversity. These major impediments are discussed below.

Ethnocentrism

A major advantage of culture is that it builds group solidarity, binding its members into a supportive, tight-knit community. Unfortunately, culture not only binds us, it can also blind us from taking different cultural perspectives. Since culture shapes thought and perception, people from the same ethnic (cultural) group run the risk of becoming *ethnocentric*—centered on their own culture to such a degree they view the world solely through their own cultural lens (frame of reference) and fail to consider or appreciate other cultural perspectives (Colombo, Cullen, & Lisle, 2013).

Optical illusions are a good example of how our particular cultural perspective can influence (and distort) our perceptions. Compare the lengths of the two lines in Figure 4.4. If you perceive the line on the right to be longer than the one on the left, your perception has been shaped by Western culture. People from Western cultures, such as Americans, perceive the line on the right to be longer. However, both lines are actually equal in length. (If you don't believe it, take out a ruler and measure them.) Interestingly, this perceptual error isn't made by people from non-Western cultures—whose living spaces and architectural structures are predominantly circular (e.g., huts or igloos)—in contrast to rectangular-shaped buildings with angled corners that typify Western cultures (Segall, Campbell, & Herskovits, 1966).

The optical illusion depicted in Figure 4.4 is just one of a number of illusions experienced by people in certain cultures, but not others (Shiraev & Levy, 2013). Cross-cultural differences in susceptibility to optical illusions illustrate

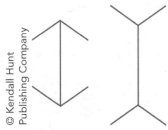

Figure 4.4
Optical Illusion

how strongly our cultural experiences can influence and sometimes misinform our perception of reality. People think they are seeing things objectively (as they actually are) but they're really seeing things subjectively—as viewed from their particular cultural perspective.

If our cultural experience can influence our perception of the physical world, it can certainly shape our perception of social events and political issues. Research in psychology indicates that the more exposure humans have to somebody or something, the more familiar it becomes and the more likely it will be perceived positively and judged favorably. The effect of familiarity is so prevalent and powerful that social psychologists have come to call it the "familiarity principle"—that is, what is familiar is perceived as better or more acceptable (Zajonc, 1968,

People whose cultural experiences involve living and working in circular structures would not be fooled by the optical illusion in Figure 4.4.

1970, 2001). Thus, we need to be mindful that the familiarity of our cultural experiences can bias us toward seeing our culture as normal or better. By remaining open to the viewpoints of people who perceive the world from different cultural vantage points, we minimize our cultural blind spots, expand our range of perception, and position ourselves to perceive the world with greater clarity and cultural sensitivity.

Stereotyping

"Stereotype" derives from two different roots: *stereo*—to look at in a fixed way—and *type*—to categorize or group together, as in the word "typical." Thus, to stereotype is to view individuals of the same type (group) in the same (fixed) way.

Stereotyping overlooks or disregards individuality; all people sharing the same group characteristic (e.g., race or gender) are viewed as having the same personal characteristics—as in the expression: "You know how they are; they're all alike." Stereotypes can also involve *bias*—literally meaning "slant"—a slant that can tilt toward the positive or the negative. Positive bias results in favorable stereotypes (e.g., "Asians are great in science and math"); negative bias leads to unfavorable stereotypes (e.g., "Asians are nerds who do nothing but study"). Here are some other examples of negative stereotypes:

* Muslims are religious terrorists.
* Whites can't jump (or dance).
* Blacks are lazy.
* Irish are alcoholics.
* Gay men are feminine; lesbian women are masculine.
* Jews are cheap.
* Women are weak.

While few people would agree with these crass stereotypes, overgeneralizations are often made about members of certain groups. Such negative overgeneralizations malign the group's reputation, rob group members of their individuality, and can weaken their self-esteem and self-confidence (as illustrated by the following experience).

When I was six years old, I was told by a six-year-old girl from a different racial group that all people of my race could not swim. Since I couldn't swim at that time and she could, I assumed she was correct. I asked a boy, who was a member of the same racial group as the girl, whether her statement was true. He responded emphatically: "Yes, it's true!" Since I was from an area where few other African Americans were around to counteract this belief about my racial group, I continued to buy into this stereotype until I finally took swimming lessons as an adult. After many lessons, I am now a lousy swimmer because I didn't even attempt to swim until I was an adult. Moral of this story: Group stereotypes can limit the confidence and potential of individual members of the stereotyped group.

—Aaron Thompson

Whether you are male or female, don't let gender stereotypes limit your career options.

1.Have you ever been stereotyped based on your appearance or group membership? If so, what was the stereotype and how did it make you feel?

2. Have you ever unintentionally perceived or treated a person in terms of a group stereotype rather than as an individual? What assumptions did you make about that person? Was that person aware of, or affected by, your stereotyping?

Prejudice

If all members of a stereotyped group are judged and evaluated in a negative way, the result is *prejudice*. The word "prejudice" literally means to "pre-judge." Typically, the pre-judgment is negative and involves *stigmatizing*—ascribing inferior or unfavorable traits to people who belong to the same group. Thus, prejudice may be defined as a negative stereotype held about a group of people that's formed before the facts are known.

People who hold a group prejudice typically avoid contact with members of that group. This enables the prejudice to continue unchallenged because there's little opportunity for the prejudiced person to have a positive experience with members of the stigmatized group that could contradict or disprove the prejudice. Thus, a vicious cycle is established in which the prejudiced person continues to avoid contact with individuals from the stigmatized group; this, in turn, continues to maintain and reinforce the prejudice.

Once prejudice has been formed, it often remains intact and resistant to change through the psychological process of *selective perception*—the tendency for biased (prejudiced) people to see what they *expect* to see and fail to see what contradicts their bias (Hugenberg & Bodenhausen, 2003). Have you ever noticed how fans rooting for their favorite sports team tend to focus on and "see" the calls of referees that go against their own team, but don't seem to react (or even notice) the calls that go against the opposing team? This is a classic example of selective perception. In effect, selective perception transforms the old adage, "seeing is believing," into "believing is seeing." This can lead prejudiced people to focus their attention on information that's consistent with their pre-judgment, causing them to "see" what supports or reinforces it and fail to see information that contradicts it.

Making matters worse, selective perception is often accompanied by *selective memory*—the tendency to remember information that's consistent with one's prejudicial belief and to forget information that's inconsistent with it or contradicts it (Judd, Ryan, & Parke, 1991). The mental processes of selective perception and selective memory often work together and often work *unconsciously*. As a result, prejudiced people may not even be aware they're using these biased mental processes or realize how these processes are keeping their prejudice permanently intact (Baron, Byrne, & Brauscombe, 2008).

"See that man over there?
Yes. Well, I hate him.
But you don't know him.
That's why I hate him."
—Gordon Allport, influential social psychologist and author of The Nature of Prejudice

We see what is behind our eyes."
—Chinese proverb

Have you witnessed selective perception or selective memory—people seeing or recalling what they believe is true (due to bias), rather than what's actually true? What happened and why do you think it happened?

Discrimination

Literally translated, the term *discrimination* means "division" or "separation." Whereas prejudice involves a belief, attitude or opinion, discrimination involves an *act* or *behavior.* Technically, discrimination can be either positive or negative. A discriminating eater may only eat healthy foods, which is a positive quality. However, discrimination is most often associated with a harmful act that results in a prejudiced person treating another individual, or group of individuals, in an unfair manner. Thus, it could be said that discrimination is prejudice put into action. For instance, to fire or not hire people on the basis of their race, gender, or sexual orientation is an act of discrimination.

Box 4.3 below contains a summary of the major forms of discrimination, prejudice, and stereotypes that have plagued humanity. As you read through the following list, place a check mark next to any item that you, a friend, or family member has experienced.

Box 4.3

Stereotypes, Prejudices, and Forms of Discrimination: A Snapshot Summary

- Ethnocentrism: viewing one's own culture or ethnic group as "central" or "normal," while viewing different cultures as "deficient" or "inferior."

  Example: Viewing another culture as "abnormal" or "uncivilized" because its members eat animals our culture views as unacceptable to eat, although we eat animals their culture views as unacceptable to eat.

- Stereotyping: viewing all (or virtually all) members of the same group in the same way—as having the same personal qualities or characteristics.

  Example: "If you're Italian, you must be in the Mafia, or have a family member who is."

- Prejudice: negative prejudgment about another group of people.

  Example: Women can't be effective leaders because they're too emotional.

- Discrimination: unequal and unfair treatment of a person or group of people—prejudice put into action.

  Example: Paying women less than men for performing the same job, even though they have the same level of education and job qualifications.

- Segregation: intentional decision made by a group to separate itself (socially or physically) from another group.

  Example: "White flight"—white people moving out of neighborhoods when people of color move in.

- Racism: belief that one's racial group is superior to another group and expressing that belief in attitude (prejudice) or action (discrimination).

> "Let us all hope that the dark clouds of racial prejudice will soon pass away and . . . in some not too distant tomorrow the radiant stars of love and brotherhood will shine over our great nation."
> —Martin Luther King, Jr., Civil rights leader, humanitarian, and youngest recipient of the Nobel Peace Prize

Box 4.3 *(Continued)*

Example: Confiscating land from American Indians based on the unfounded belief that they are "uncivilized" or "savages."

- Institutional Racism: racial discrimination rooted in organizational policies and practices that disadvantage certain racial groups.

  Example: Race-based discrimination in mortgage lending, housing, and bank loans.

- Racial Profiling: investigating or arresting someone solely on the basis of the person's race, ethnicity, or national origin—without witnessing actual criminal behavior or possessing incriminating evidence.

  Example: Police making a traffic stop or conducting a personal search based solely on an individual's racial features.

- Slavery: forced labor in which people are considered to be property, held against their will, and deprived of the right to receive wages.

  Example: Enslavement of Blacks, which was legal in the United States until 1865.

- "Jim Crow" Laws: formal and informal laws created by whites to segregate Blacks after the abolition of slavery.

  Example: Laws in certain parts of the United States that once required Blacks to use separate bathrooms and be educated in separate schools.

- Apartheid: an institutionalized system of "legal racism" supported by a nation's government. (Apartheid derives from a word in the Afrikaan language, meaning "apartness.")

  Example: South Africa's national system of racial segregation and discrimination that was in place from 1948 to 1994.

> Never, never, and never again shall it be that this beautiful land will again experience the oppression of one by another."
> —Nelson Mandela, anti-apartheid revolutionary, first Black president of South Africa after apartheid, and winner of the Nobel Peace Prize

- Hate Crimes: criminal action motivated solely by prejudice toward the crime victim.

  Example: Acts of vandalism or assault aimed at members of a particular ethnic group or persons of a particular sexual orientation.

- Hate Groups: organizations whose primary purpose is to stimulate prejudice, discrimination, or aggression

toward certain groups of people based on their ethnicity, race, religion, etc.

Example: The Ku Klux Klan—an American terrorist group that perpetrates hatred toward all non-white races.

- Genocide: mass murdering of a particular ethnic or racial group.

  Example: The Holocaust, in which millions of Jews were systematically murdered during World War II. Other examples include the murdering of Cambodians under the Khmer Rouge regime, the murdering of Bosnian Muslims in the former country of Yugoslavia, and the slaughter of the Tutsi minority by the Hutu majority in Rwanda.

- Classism: prejudice or discrimination based on social class, particularly toward people of lower socioeconomic status.

  Example: Acknowledging the contributions made by politicians and wealthy industrialists to America, while ignoring the contributions of poor immigrants, farmers, slaves, and pioneer women.

- Religious Intolerance: denying the fundamental human right of people to hold religious beliefs, or to hold religious beliefs that differ from one's own.

  Example: An atheist who forces nonreligious (secular) beliefs on others, or a member of a religious group who believes that people who hold different religious beliefs are infidels or "sinners" whose souls will not be saved.

> Rivers, ponds, lakes and streams—they all have different names, but they all contain water. Just as religions do—they all contain truths."
> —Muhammad Ali, three-time world heavyweight boxing champion, member of the International Boxing Hall of Fame, and recipient of the Spirit of America Award as the most recognized American in the world

- Anti-Semitism: prejudice or discrimination toward Jews or people who practice the religion of Judaism.

  Example: Disliking Jews because they're the ones who "killed Christ."

- Xenophobia: fear or hatred of foreigners, outsiders, or strangers.

(continued)

Box 4.3 (*Continued*)

Example: Believing that immigrants should be banned from entering the country because they'll undermine our economy and increase our crime rate.

- Regional Bias: prejudice or discrimination based on the geographical region in which an individual is born and raised.

  Example: A northerner thinking that all southerners are racists.

- Jingoism: excessive interest and belief in the superiority of one's own nation—without acknowledging its mistakes or weaknesses—often accompanied by an aggressive foreign policy that neglects the needs of other nations or the common needs of all nations.

  Example: "Blind patriotism"—failure to see the shortcomings of one's own nation and viewing any questioning or criticism of one's own nation as being disloyal or "unpatriotic." (As in the slogan, "America: right or wrong" or "America: love it or leave it!")

  > Above all nations is humanity."
  > —Motto of the University of Hawaii

- Terrorism: intentional acts of violence committed against civilians that are motivated by political or religious prejudice.

Example: The September 11, 2001, attacks on the United States.

- Sexism: prejudice or discrimination based on sex or gender.

  Example: Believing that women should not pursue careers in fields traditionally filled only by men (e.g., engineering or politics) because they lack the innate qualities or natural skills to do so.

- Heterosexism: belief that heterosexuality is the only acceptable sexual orientation.

  Example: Believing that gays should not have the same legal rights and opportunities as heterosexuals.

- Homophobia: extreme fear or hatred of homosexuals.

  Example: Creating or contributing to anti-gay websites, or "gay bashing" (acts of violence toward gays).

- Ageism: prejudice or discrimination toward certain age groups, particularly toward the elderly.

  Example: Believing that all "old" people have dementia and shouldn't be allowed to drive or make important decisions.

- Ableism: prejudice or discrimination toward people who are disabled or handicapped (physically, mentally, or emotionally).

  Example: Intentionally avoiding social contact with people in wheelchairs.

REFLECTION

As you read through the above list, did you, a friend, or family member experience any of the form(s) of prejudice listed?

If yes, what happened and why do you think it happened?

Strategies for Overcoming Stereotypes and Prejudices

We may hold prejudices, stereotypes, or subtle biases that bubble beneath the surface of our conscious awareness. The following practices and strategies can help us become more aware of our unconscious biases and relate more effectively to individuals from diverse groups.

Consciously avoid preoccupation with physical appearances. Remember the old proverb: "It's what inside that counts." Judge others by the quality of their inner qualities, not by the familiarity of their outer features. Get beneath the superficial surface of appearances and relate to people not in terms of how they look but who they are and how they act.

Form impressions of others on a person-to-person basis, not on the basis of their group membership. This may seem like an obvious and easy thing to do, but research shows that humans have a natural tendency to perceive individuals from unfamiliar groups as being more alike (or all alike) than members of their own group (Taylor, Peplau, & Sears, 2006). Thus, we need to remain mindful of this tendency and make a conscious effort to perceive and treat individuals of diverse groups as unique human beings, not according to some general (stereotypical) rule of thumb.

Note

It's valuable to learn about different cultures and the common characteristics shared by members of the same culture; however, this shouldn't be done while ignoring individual differences. Don't assume that all individuals who share the same cultural background share the same personal characteristics.

(Review your results from the My MI Advantage Inventory. How might the recommendations you received about your interpersonal skills enable you to become more adept at connecting with people from cultural backgrounds that are different from your own?)

Strategies for Increasing Interpersonal Contact and Interaction with Members of Diverse Groups

Place yourself in situations and locations on campus where you will come in regular contact with individuals from diverse groups. Distancing ourselves from diversity ensures we'll never experience diversity and benefit from it. Research in social psychology shows that relationships are more likely to form among people who come in regular contact with

> I grew up in a very racist family. Even just a year ago, I could honestly say 'I hate Asians' with a straight face and mean it. My senior AP language teacher tried hard to teach me not to be judgmental. He got me to be open to others, so much so that my current boyfriend is half Chinese."
> —First-year college student

> Stop judging by mere appearances, and make a right judgment."
> —Bible, John 7:24

> You can't judge a book by the cover."
> —1962 hit song by Elias Bates, a.k.a. Bo Diddley (Note: a "bo diddley" is a one-stringed African guitar)

REFLECTION

Your comfort level while interacting with people from diverse groups is likely to depend on how much prior experience you've had with members of those groups. Rate the amount or variety of diversity you have experienced in the following settings:

1.	The high school you attended	high	moderate	low
2.	The college or university you now attend	high	moderate	low
3.	The neighborhood in which you grew up	high	moderate	low
4.	Places where you have been employed	high	moderate	low

Which setting had the most and the least diversity?

What do you think accounted for this difference?

one another (Latané, et al., 1995), and research on diversity reveals that when there's regular contact between members of different racial or ethnic groups, stereotyping is sharply reduced and intercultural friendships are more likely to develop (Pettigrew, 1997, 1998). You can create these conditions by making an intentional attempt to sit near diverse students in the classroom, library, or student café, and by joining them for class discussion groups or group projects.

Take advantage of social media to "chat" virtually with students from diverse groups on your own campus, or students on other campuses. Electronic communication can be a convenient and comfortable way to initially interact with members of diverse groups with whom you have had little prior experience. After interacting *online*, you're more likely to feel more comfortable about interacting *in person*.

Engage in co-curricular experiences involving diversity. Review your student handbook to find co-curricular programs, student activities, student clubs, or campus organizations that emphasize diversity awareness and appreciation. Studies indicate that participation in co-curricular experiences relating to diversity promotes critical thinking (Pascarella & Terenzini, 2005) and reduces unconscious prejudice (Blair, 2002).

Consider spending time at the multicultural center on your campus, or joining a campus club or organization that's devoted to diversity awareness (e.g., multicultural or international student club). Putting yourself in these situations will enable you to make regular contact with members of cultural groups other than your own; it also sends a clear message to members of these groups that you value their culture because you've taken the initiative to connect with them on "their turf."

If your campus sponsors multicultural or cross-cultural retreats, strongly consider participating in them. A retreat setting can provide a comfortable environment in which you can interact personally with diverse students without being distracted by your customary social circle and daily routine.

If possible, participate in a study abroad or travel study program that gives you the opportunity to live in another country and interact directly with its native citizens. In addition to coursework, you can gain international knowledge and a global perspective by participating in programs that enable you to actually *experience* a different country. You can do this for a full term or for a shorter time period (e.g., January, May, or summer term). To prepare for international experiences, take a course in the language, culture, or history of the nation to which you will be traveling.

Research on students who participate in study abroad programs indicates that these experiences promote greater appreciation of cross-cultural differences, greater interest in world affairs, and greater commitment to peace and international cooperation (Bok, 2006; Kaufmann, et al., 1992). Additional research shows that study abroad benefits students' personal development, including improved self-confidence, sense of independence, and ability to function in complex environments (Carlson, et al., 1990; IES Abroad News, 2002).

Incorporate diversity courses into your planned schedule of classes. Review your college catalog (bulletin) and identify courses that are designed to promote understanding or appreciation of diversity. These courses may focus on diverse cultures found within the United States (sometimes referred to as multicultural courses) or diverse cultures associated with different countries (sometimes referred to as international or cross-cultural courses).

In a national study of college students who experienced multicultural courses, it was discovered that students of all racial and ethnic groups made significant gains in learning and intellectual development (Smith, 1997; Smith, et al., 1997).

Taking courses focusing on international diversity can help you develop the global perspective needed for success in today's international economy and enhance the quality of your college transcript (Brooks, 2009; Cuseo, et al., 2013; National Association of Colleges & Employers, 2003).

Be on the lookout for diversity implications associated with topics you're reading about or discussing in class. Consider the multicultural and cross-cultural ramifications of material you're studying and use examples of diversity to support or illustrate your points. If you're allowed to choose a topic for a research project, select one that relates to diversity or has implications for diversity.

Seek out the views and opinions of classmates from diverse backgrounds. Discussions among students of different races and cultures can reduce prejudice and promote intercultural appreciation, but only if each member's cultural identity and perspective is sought out and valued by members of the discussion group (Baron, Byrne, & Brauscombe, 2008). During class discussions, you can demonstrate leadership by seeking out views and opinions of classmates from diverse backgrounds and ensuring that the ideas of people from minority groups are included and respected. Also, after class discussions, you can ask students from different backgrounds if there was any point made or position taken in class that they would have strongly questioned or challenged.

If there is little or no diversity among students in class, encourage your classmates to look at topics from diverse perspectives. For instance, you might ask: "If there were international students here, what might they be adding to our discussion?" or, "If members of certain minority groups were here, would they be offering a different viewpoint?"

If you are given the opportunity to form your own discussion groups and group project teams, join or create groups composed of students from diverse backgrounds. You can gain greater exposure to diverse perspectives by intentionally joining or forming learning groups with students who differ in terms of gender, age, race, or ethnicity. Including diversity in your discussion groups not only creates social variety, it also enhances the quality of your group's work by allowing members to gain access to and learn from multiple perspectives. For instance, in learning groups comprised of students that are diverse with respect to age, older students will bring a broad range of life experiences that younger students can draw upon and learn from, while younger students can provide a more contemporary and idealistic perspective to the group's discussions. Gender diversity is also likely to infuse group discussions with different learning styles and approaches to understanding issues. Studies show that males are more likely to be "separate knowers"—they tend to "detach" themselves from the concept or issue being discussed so they can analyze it. In contrast, females are more likely to be "connected knowers"—they tend to relate personally to concepts and connect them with their own experiences and the experiences of others. For example, when interpreting a poem, males are more likely to ask: "What techniques can I use to analyze it?" In contrast, females would be more likely to ask: "What is the poet trying to say to me?" (Belenky, et al., 1986). It's also been found that females are more likely to work collaboratively during group discussions and collect the ideas of other members; in contrast, males are more likely to adopt a competitive approach and debate the ideas of others (Magolda, 1992). Both of these styles of learning are valuable and you can capitalize on these different styles by forming gender-diverse discussion groups.

Form collaborative learning teams with students from diverse backgrounds. A learning *team* is more than a discussion group that tosses around ideas; it moves beyond discussion to *collaboration*—its members "co-labor" (work together) to reach the same goal. Research from kindergarten through college indicates that when students collaborate in teams, their academic performance and interpersonal skills are strengthened (Cuseo, 1996). Also, when individuals from different racial groups work collaboratively toward the same goal, racial prejudice is reduced and interracial friendships are more likely to be formed (Allport, 1954; Amir, 1976; Brown, et al., 2003; Dovidio, Eller, & Hewstone, 2011). These positive developments may be explained, in part, by the fact that when members of diverse groups come together on the same team, nobody is a member of an "out" group ("them"); instead, everybody belongs to the same "in" group ("us") (Pratto, et al., 2000; Sidanius, et al., 2000).

In an analysis of multiple studies involving more than 90,000 people from 25 different countries, it was found that when interaction between members of diverse groups took place under the conditions described in Box 4.4, prejudice was significantly reduced (Pettigrew & Tropp, 2000) and the greatest gains in learning took place (Johnson, Johnson, & Smith, 1998; Slavin, 1995).

Box 4.4

Tips for Teamwork: Creating Diverse and Effective Learning Teams

1. Intentionally form learning teams with students who have different cultural backgrounds and life experiences. Teaming up only with friends or classmates whose backgrounds and experiences are similar to yours can actually impair your team's performance because teammates can get off track and onto topics that have nothing to do with the learning task (e.g., what they did last weekend or what they're planning to do next weekend).

2. Before jumping into group work, take some time to interact informally with your teammates. When team members have some social "warm up" time (e.g., time to learn each other's names and learn something about each other), they feel more comfortable expressing their ideas and are more likely to develop a stronger sense of team identity. This feeling of group solidarity can create a foundation of trust among group members, enabling them to work together as a team, particularly if they come from diverse (and unfamiliar) cultural backgrounds.

    The context in which a group interacts can influence the openness and harmony of their interaction. Group members are more likely to interact openly and collaboratively when they work in a friendly, informal environment that's conducive to relationship building. A living room or a lounge area provides a warmer and friendlier team-learning atmosphere than a sterile classroom.

3. Have teammates work together to complete a single work product. One jointly created product serves to highlight the team's collaborative effort and collective achievement (e.g., a completed sheet of answers to questions, or a comprehensive list of ideas). Creating a common final product helps keep individuals thinking in terms of "we" (not "me") and keeps the team moving in the same direction toward the same goal.

4. Group members should work interdependently—they should depend on each other to reach their common goal and each member should have equal opportunity to contribute to the team's final product. Each teammate should take responsibility for making an indispensable contribution to the team's end product, such as contributing: (a) a different piece of *information* (e.g., a specific chapter from the textbook or a particular section of class notes), (b) a particular form of *thinking* to the learning task (e.g., analysis, synthesis, or application), or (c) a different *perspective* (e.g., national, international, or global). Said in another way, each group member should assume personal responsibility for a piece that's needed to complete the whole puzzle.

    Similar to a sports team, each member of a learning team should have a specific role to play. For instance, each teammate could perform one of the following roles:

    - manager—whose role is to assure that the team stays on track and keeps moving toward its goal;
    - moderator—whose role is to ensure that all teammates have equal opportunity to contribute;
    - summarizer—whose role is to monitor the team's progress, identifying what has been accomplished and what still needs to be done;
    - recorder—whose role is to keep a written record of the team's ideas.

5. After concluding work in diverse learning teams, take time to reflect on the experience. The final step in any learning process, whether it be learning from a lecture or learning from a group discussion, is to step back from the process and thoughtfully review it. Deep learning requires not only effortful action but also thoughtful reflection (Bligh, 2000; Roediger, Dudai, & Fitzpatrick, 2007). You can reflect on your experiences with diverse learning groups by asking yourself questions that prompt you to process the ideas shared by members of your group and the impact those ideas had on you. For instance, ask yourself (and your teammates) the following questions:

    - What major similarities in viewpoints did all group members share? (What were the common themes?)
    - What major differences of opinion were expressed by diverse members of our group? (What were the variations on the themes?)
    - Were there particular topics or issues raised during the discussion that provoked intense reactions or emotional responses from certain members of our group?
    - Did the group discussion lead any individuals to change their mind about an idea or position they originally held?

    When contact among people from diverse groups takes place under the five conditions described in this box, group work is transformed into *teamwork* and promotes higher levels of thinking and deeper appreciation of diversity. A win–win scenario is created: Learning and thinking are strengthened while bias and prejudice are weakened (Allport, 1979; Amir, 1969; Aronson, Wilson, & Akert, 2013; Cook, 1984; Sherif, et al., 1961).

Have you had an experience with a member of an unfamiliar racial or cultural group that caused you to change your attitude or viewpoint toward that group?

Take a stand against prejudice or discrimination by constructively disagreeing with students who make stereotypical statements and prejudicial remarks. By saying nothing, you may avoid conflict, but your silence may be perceived by others to mean that you agree with the person who made the prejudicial remark. Studies show that when members of the same group observe another member of their own group making prejudicial comments, prejudice tends to increase among all group members—probably due to peer pressure of group conformity (Stangor, Sechrist, & Jost, 2001). In contrast, if a person's prejudicial remark is challenged by a member of one's own group, particularly a fellow member who is liked and respected, that person's prejudice decreases along with similar prejudices held by other members of the group (Baron, Byrne, & Brauscombe, 2008). Thus, by taking a leadership role and challenging peers who make prejudicial remarks, you're likely to reduce that person's prejudice as well as the prejudice of others who hear the remark. In addition, you help create a campus climate in which students experience greater satisfaction with their college experience and are more likely to complete their college degree. Studies show that a campus climate which is hostile toward students from minority groups lowers students' level of college satisfaction and college completion rates of both minority and majority students (Cabrera, et al., 1999; Eimers & Pike, 1997; Nora & Cabrera, 1996).

Note

By actively opposing prejudice on campus, you demonstrate diversity leadership and moral character. You become a role model whose actions send a clear message that valuing diversity is not only the smart thing to do, it's the right thing to do.

If you heard another student telling an insulting racial or gender joke, do you think you would do anything about it? Why?

Chapter Summary and Highlights

Diversity refers to the variety of groups that comprise humanity (the human species). Humans differ from one another in multiple ways, including physical features, religious beliefs, mental and physical abilities, national origins, social backgrounds, gender, and sexual orientation. Diversity involves the important political issue of securing equal rights and social justice for all people; however, it's also an important *educational* issue—an integral element of the college experience that enriches learning, personal development, and career preparation.

When a group of people share the same traditions and customs, it creates a culture that serves to bind people into a supportive, tight-knit community. However, culture can also lead its members to view the world solely through their own cultural lens (known as ethnocentrism), which can blind them to other cultural perspectives. Ethnocentrism can contribute to stereotyping—viewing individual members of another cultural group in the same (fixed) way, in which they're seen as having similar personal characteristics.

Stereotyping can result in prejudice—a biased prejudgment about another person or group of people that's formed before the facts are known. Stereotyping and prejudice often go hand in hand because if the stereotype is negative, members of the stereotyped group are then judged negatively. Discrimination takes prejudice one step further by converting the negative prejudgment into behavior that results in unfair treatment of others. Thus, discrimination is prejudice put into action.

Once stereotyping and prejudice are overcome, we are positioned to experience diversity and reap its multiple benefits—which include sharper self-awareness, deeper learning, higher-level thinking, and better career preparation.

The increasing diversity of students on campus, combined with the wealth of diversity-related educational experiences found in the college curriculum and co-curriculum, presents you with an unprecedented opportunity to infuse diversity into your college experience. Seize this opportunity and capitalize on the power of diversity to increase the quality of your college education and your prospects for success in the 21st century.

Learning More through the World Wide Web:

Internet-Based Resources

For additional information on diversity, see the following websites:

Stereotyping:
ReducingStereotypeThreat.org at www.reducingstereotypethreat.org

Prejudice and Discrimination:
Southern Poverty Law Center at www.splcenter.org/

Human Rights:
Amnesty International at www.amnesty.org/en/discrimination
Center for Economic & Social Justice at www.cesj.org

Sexism in the Media:
"Killing Us Softly" at www.youtube.com/watch?v=PTlmho_RovY

LGBT Acceptance and Support:
"It Gets Better Project," at www.itgetsbetter.org

References

Acredolo, C., & O'Connor, J. (1991). On the difficulty of detecting cognitive uncertainty. *Human Development, 34*, 204–223.

Allport, G. W. (1954). *The nature of prejudice.* Cambridge, MA: Addison-Wesley.

Allport, G. W. (1979). *The nature of prejudice* (3rd ed.). Reading, MA: Addison-Wesley.

Amir, Y. (1969). Contact hypothesis in ethnic relations. *Psychological Bulletin, 71*, 319–342.

Amir, Y. (1976). The role of intergroup contact in change of prejudice and ethnic relations. In P. A. Katz (Ed.), *Towards the elimination of racism* (pp. 245–308). New York: Pergamon Press.

Anderson, M., & Fienberg, S. (2000). Race and ethnicity and the controversy over the US Census. *Current Sociology, 48*(3), 87–110.

Aronson, E., Wilson, T. D., & Akert, R. M. (2013). *Social psychology* (8th ed.). Upper Saddle River, NJ: Pearson/Prentice Hall.

Association of American Colleges & Universities (AAC&U). (2002). *Greater expectations: A new vision for learning as a nation goes to college.* Washington, DC: Author.

Association of American Colleges & Universities (AAC&U). (2004). *Our students' best work.* Washington, DC: Author.

Baron, et. al. (2008). *Social psychology* (12th ed). Boston, MA: Allyn & Bacon.

Belenky, M. F., Clinchy, B., Goldberger, N. R., & Tarule, J. M. (1986). *Women's ways of knowing: The development of self, voice, and mind.* New York: Basic Books.

Blair, I. V. (2002). The malleability of automatic stereotypes and prejudice. *Personality and Social Psychology Review, 6*(3), 242–261.

Bligh, D. A. (2000). *What's the use of lectures?* San Francisco: Jossey Bass.

Bok, D. (2006). *Our underachieving colleges: A candid look at how much students learn and why they should be learning more.* Princeton, NJ: Princeton University Press.

Bridgeman, B. (2003). *Psychology and evolution: The origins of mind.* Thousand Oaks, CA: Sage Publications.

Bronfenbrenner, U. (Ed.). (2005). *Making human beings human: Bioecological perspectives on human development.* Thousand Oaks, CA: Sage.

Brookfield, S. D. (1987). *Developing critical thinkers.* San Francisco, CA: Jossey-Bass.

Brooks, I. (2009). *Organisational behaviour* (4th ed.). Englewood Cliffs, NJ: Prentice Hall.

Brown, T. D., Dane, F. C., & Durham, M. D. (1998). Perception of race and ethnicity. *Journal of Social Behavior and Personality, 13*(2), 295–306.

Brown, K. T., Brown, T. N., Jackson, J. S., Sellers, R. M., & Manuel, W. J. (2003). Teammates on and off the field? Contact with Black teammates and the racial attitudes of White student athletes. *Journal of Applied Social Psychology, 33*, 1379–1403.

Cabrera, A., Nora, A., Terenzini, P., Pascarella, E., & Hagedorn, L. S. (1999). Campus racial climate and the adjustment of students to college: A comparison between White students and African American students. *The Journal of Higher Education, 70*(2), 134–160.

Caplan, P. J., & Caplan, J. B. (2008). *Thinking critically about research on sex and gender* (3rd ed.). New York: HarperCollins College Publishers.

Carlson, et al. (1990). Individual differences in the behavioral effects of stressors attributable to lateralized differences in mesocortical dopamine systems. *Society for Neuroscience Abstracts, 16*, 233.

Ciancotto, J. (2005). *Hispanic and Latino same-sex couple households in the United States: A report from the 2000 Census.* New York: The National Gay and Lesbian Task Force Policy Institute and the National Latino/a Coalition for Justice.

Colombo, G., Cullen, R., & Lisle, B. (2013). *Rereading America: Cultural contexts for critical thinking and writing* (9th ed.). Boston, MA: Bedford Books of St. Martin's Press.

Cook, S. W. (1984). Cooperative interaction in multiethnic contexts. In N. Miller & M. B. Brewer (Eds.), *Groups in contact: The psychology of desegregation* (pp. 291–302). New York: Academic Press.

Cuseo, J. B. (1996). *Cooperative learning: A pedagogy for addressing contemporary challenges and critical issues in higher education.* Stillwater, OK: New Forums Press.

Cuseo, J. B., et al. (2013). *Thriving in community college & beyond: Strategies for academic success and personal development.* Dubuque, IA: Kendall Hunt Publishing Company.

DeNavas-Walt, C., Proctor, B. D., & Smith, J. C. (2013). *Income, poverty, and health insurance coverage in the United States, 2012.* U.S. Census Bureau, Current Population Reports, P60-245, Washington, DC: U.S. Government Printing Office.

Dessel, A. (2012). Effects of intergroup dialogue: Public school teachers and sexual orientation prejudice. *Small Group Research, 41*(5), 556–592.

Dolan, M., & Romney, L. (2015, June 27). "Law in California is now a right for all." *Los Angeles Times*, pp. A1, A8.

Donald, J. G. (2002). *Learning to think: Disciplinary perspectives.* San Francisco: Jossey-Bass.

Dovidio, J. F., Eller, A., & Hewstone, M. (2011). Improving intergroup relations through direct, extended and other forms of indirect contact. *Group Processes & Intergroup Relations, 14*, 147–160.

Dryden, G., & Vos, J. (1999). *The learning revolution: To change the way the world learns.* Torrance, CA and Auckland, New Zealand: The Learning Web.

Education Commission of the States. (1995). *Making quality count in undergraduate education.* Denver, CO: ECS Distribution Center.

Education Commission of the States. (1996). *Bridging the gap between neuroscience and education.* Denver, CO: Author.

Eimers, M. T., & Pike, G. R. (1997). Minority and nonminority adjustment to college: Differences or similarities. *Research in Higher Education, 38*(1), 77–97.

Erickson, B. L., Peters, C. B., & Strommer, D. W. (2006). *Teaching first-year college students.* San Francisco: Jossey-Bass.

Family Care Foundation. (2015). *If the world were a village of 100 people.* Retrieved from http://www.familycare.org/special-interest/if-the-world-were-a-village-of-100-people/.

Feagin, J. R., & Feagin, C. B. (2007). *Racial and ethnic relations* (8th ed.). Englewood Cliffs, NJ: Prentice Hall.

Fixman, C. S. (1990). The foreign language needs of U.S. based corporations. *Annals of the American Academy of Political and Social Science, 511*, 25–46.

Friedman, T. L. (2005). *The world is flat: A brief history of the twenty-first century: Revitalizing the civic mission of schools.* Alexandria, VA: Farrar, Strauss & Giroux.

Gorski, P. C. (1995–2009). *Key characteristics of a multicultural curriculum.* Critical Multicultural Pavilion: Multicultural Curriculum Reform (An EdChange Project). Retrieved from www.edchange.org/multicultural/curriculum/characteristics.html.

Gould, E. & Wething, H. (2013). Health care, the market and consumer choice. *Inquiry, 50*(1), 85–86.

Gurin, P. (1999). New research on the benefits of diversity in college and beyond: An empirical analysis. *Diversity Digest* (spring). Retrieved from http://www.diversityweb.org/Digest/Sp99/benefits.html.

Harris, A. (2010). Leading system transformation. *School Leadership and Management, 30* (July).

Hart Research Associates. (2013). *It takes more than a major: Employer priorities for college learning and student success.* Washington, DC: Author.

HERI (Higher Education Research Institute). (2013). *Your first college year survey 2012.* Los Angeles, CA: Cooperative Institutional Research Program, University of California-Los Angeles.

HERI (Higher Education Research Institute). (2014). *Your first college year survey 2014.* Los Angeles, CA: Cooperative Institutional Research Program, University of California-Los Angeles.

Hugenberg, K., & Bodenhausen, G. V. (2003). Facing prejudice: Implicit prejudice and the perception of facial threat. *Psychological Science, 14*, 640–643.

IES Abroad News. (2002). *Study abroad: A lifetime of benefits.* Retrieved from www.iesabroad.org/study-abroad/news/study-abroad-lifetime-benefits.

Jablonski, N. G., & Chaplin, G. (2002). Skin deep. *Scientific American, (October)*, 75–81.

Johnson, D., Johnson, R., & Smith, K. (1998). Cooperative learning returns to college: What evidence is there that it works? *Change, 30*, 26–35.

Judd, C. M., Ryan, C. S., & Parke, B. (1991). Accuracy in the judgment of in-group and out-group variability. *Journal of Personality and Social Psychology, 61*, 366–379.

Kaufmann, N. L., Martin, J. M., & Weaver, H. D. (1992). *Students abroad: Strangers at home: Education for a global society.* Yarmouth, ME: Intercultural Press.

Kelly, K. (1994). *Out of control: The new biology of machines, social systems, and the economic world.* Reading, MA: Addison-Wesley.

Kitchener, K., Wood, P., & Jensen, L. (2000, August). *Curricular, co-curricular, and institutional influence on real-world problem-solving.* Paper presented at the annual meeting of the American Psychological Association, Boston.

Kochlar, R., Fry, R., & Taylor, P. (2011). Wealth gaps rise to record highs between Whites, Blacks, Hispanics, twenty-to-one. *Pew Research Social and Demographics Trends* (July). Retrieved from http://www.pewsocialtrends.org/2011/07/26/wealth-gaps-rise-to-record-highs-between-whites-blacks-hispanics/

Lancaster, L., et al. (2002). *When generations collide: Who they are. Why they clash.* New York: HarperCollins.

Latané, B., Liu, J. H., Nowak, A., Bonevento, N., & Zheng, L. (1995). Distance matters: Physical space and social impact. *Personality and Social Psychology Bulletin, 21*, 795–805.

Leung, A. K., Maddux, W. W., Galinsky, A. D., & Chie-yue, C. (2008). Multicultural experience enhances creativity: The when and how. *American Psychologist, 63*(3), 169–181.

Lewis, M., Paul, G. W., & Fennig, C. D. (Eds). (2014). *Ethnologue: Languages of the world* (17th ed.). Dallas, TX: SIL International. Online version: http://www.ethnologue.com.

Luhman, R. (2007). *The sociological outlook*. Lanham, MD: Rowman & Littlefield.

Maddux, W. W. & Galinsky, A. D. (2009). Cultural borders and mental barriers: the relationship between living abroad and creativity. *Journal of Personality and Social Psychology, 96*(5), 1047–1061.

Magolda, M. B. B. (1992). *Knowing and reasoning in college*. San Francisco, CA: Jossey-Bass.

Mendez, F., Krahn, T., Schrack, B., Krahn, A. M., Veeramah, K., Woerner, A., Fomine, F. L. M., Bradman, N., Thomas, M., Karafet, T., & Hammer, M. (2013). An African American paternal lineage adds an extremely ancient root to the human Y chromosome phylogenetic tree. *The American Journal of Human Genetics, 92*, 454–459.

Meredith, M. (2011). *Born in Africa: The quest for the origins of human life*. New York: Public Affairs.

Nagda, B. R., Gurin, P., & Johnson, S. M. (2005). Living, doing and thinking diversity: How does pre-college diversity experience affect first-year students' engagement with college diversity? In R. S. Feldman (Ed.), *Improving the first year of college: Research and practice* (pp. 73–110). Mahwah, NJ: Lawrence Erlbaum.

Nathan, R. (2005). *My freshman year: What a professor learned by becoming a student*. London: Penguin.

National Association of Colleges and Employers (NACE). (2003). *Job outlook 2003 survey*. Bethlehem, PA: Author.

National Association of Colleges & Employers. (2014). *Job Outlook 2014 survey*. Bethlehem, PA: Author.

National Center for Education Statistics. (2011). *Digest of education statistics, table 237. Total fall enrollment in degree-granting institutions, by level of student, sex, attendance status, and race/ethnicity: Selected years, 1976 through 2010*. Alexandria, VA: U.S. Department of Education. Retrieved from http://neces.ed/gov/programs/digest/d11/tables/dt11_237.asp.

National Survey of Women Voters. (1998). *Autumn overview report conducted by DYG Inc.* Retrieved from http:www.diversityweb.org/research_and_trends/research_evaluation_impact_/campus_community_connections/ national_poll.cfm.

Nhan, D. (2012). "Census: Minorities constitute 37 percent of U.S. population." *National Journal: The Next America—Demographics 2012*. Retrieved from http:www.nationaljournal.com/thenextamerica/demographics/census-minorities-constitute-37-percent-of-u-s-population-20120517.

Nora, A., & Cabrera, A. (1996). The role of perceptions of prejudice and discrimination on the adjustment of minority college students. *The Journal of Higher Education, 67*(2), 119–148.

Office of Research. (1994). *What employers expect of college graduates: International knowledge and second language skills*. Washington, DC: Office of Educational Research and Improvement, U.S. Department of Education.

Olson, L. (2007). What does "ready" mean? *Education Week, 40*, 7–12.

Pascarella, E. T. (2001, November/December). Cognitive growth in college: Surprising and reassuring findings from the National Study of Student Learning. *Change*, 21–27.

Pascarella, E. T., & Terenzini, P. T. (2005). *How college affects students: A third decade of research* (Vol. 2). San Francisco, CA: Jossey-Bass.

Pascarella, E., Palmer, B., Moye, M., & Pierson, C. (2001). Do diversity experiences influence the development of critical thinking? *Journal of College Student Development, 42*(3), 257–291.

Peoples, J., & Bailey, G. (2011). *Humanity: An introduction to cultural anthropology*. Belmont, CA: Wadsworth, Cengage Learning. Retrieved from http://www.aacu.org/leap/documents/2009-employersurvey.pdf.

Pettigrew, T. F. (1997). Generalized intergroup contact effects on prejudice. *Personality and Social Psychology Bulletin, 23*, 173–185.

Pettigrew, T. F. (1998). Intergroup contact theory. *Annual Review of Psychology, 49*, 65–85.

Pettigrew, T. F., & Tropp, L. R. (2000). Does intergroup contact reduce prejudice? Recent meta-analytic findings. In S. Oskamp (Ed.), *Reducing prejudice and discrimination* (pp. 93–114). Mahwah, NJ: Lawrence Erlbaum Associates.

Pinker, S. (2000). *The language instinct: The new science of language and mind*. New York: Perennial.

Pratto, F., Liu, J. H., Levin, S., Sidanius, J., Shih, M., Bachrach, H., & Hegarty, P. (2000). Social dominance orientation and the legitimization of inequality across cultures. *Journal of Cross-Cultural Psychology, 31*, 369–409.

Reid, G. B. R., & Hetherington, R. (2010). *The climate connection: Climate change and modern evolution*. Cambridge, UK: Cambridge University Press.

Roediger, H. L., Dudai, Y., & Fitzpatrick, S. M. (2007). *Science of memory: concepts*. New York, NY: Oxford University Press.

Shah, A. (2009). *Global issues: Poverty facts and stats*. Retrieved from http://www.globalissues.org/artoc;e/26/poverty-facts-and-stats.

Sherif, M., Harvey, D. J., White, B. J., Hood, W. R., & Sherif, C. W. (1961). *The Robbers' cave experiment*. Norman, OK: Institute of Group Relations.

Shiraev, E. D., & Levy, D. (2013). *Cross-cultural psychology: Critical thinking and contemporary applications* (5th ed.). Upper Saddle River, NJ: Pearson Education.

Sidanius, J., Levin, S., Liu, H., & Pratto, F. (2000). Social dominance orientation, anti-egalitarianism, and the political psychology of gender: An extension and cross-cultural replication. *European Journal of Social Psychology, 30*, 41–67.

Slavin, R. E. (1995). *Cooperative learning* (2nd ed.). Boston: Allyn & Bacon.

Smith, D. (1997). How diversity influences learning. *Liberal Education, 83*(2), 42–48.

Smith, D. G., Guy, L., Gerbrick, G. L., Figueroa, M. A., Watkins, G. H., Levitan, T., Moore, L. C., Merchant, P. A., Beliak, H. D., & Figueroa, B. (1997). *Diversity works: The emerging picture of how students benefit.* Washington, DC: Association of American Colleges and Universities.

Stangor, C., Sechrist, G. B., & Jost, J. T. (2001). Changing racial beliefs by providing consensus information. *Personality and Social Psychology Bulletin, 27*, 484–494.

Stoltz, P. G. (2014). *Grit: The new science of what it takes to persevere, flourish, succeed.* San Luis Obispo: Climb Strong Press.

Taylor, S. E., Peplau, L. A., & Sears, D. O. (2006). *Social psychology* (12th ed.). Upper Saddle River, NJ: Pearson/Prentice-Hall.

Thompson, A., & Cuseo, J. (2014). *Diversity and the college experience.* Dubuque, IA: Kendall Hunt.

U.S. Census Bureau. (2008). *Bureau of Labor Statistics.* Washington, DC: Author.

United States Census Bureau. (2013a, July 8). *About race.* Retrieved from http://www.census.gov/topics/population/race/about.html.

U.S. Census Bureau. (2013b). *Poverty.* Retrieved from https://www.census.gov/hhes/www/poverty/data/threshld/.

United States Census Bureau. (2015, March). *Projections of the size and composition of the U.S. population: 2014 to 2060.* Retrieved from http://www.census.gov/content/dam/Census/library/publications/2015/demo/p25-1143.pdf.

Wabash National Study of Liberal Arts Education. (2007). *Liberal arts outcomes.* Retrieved from http:www.liberalarts.wabash.edu/ study-overview/.

Wheelright, J. (2005, March). Human, study thyself. *Discover*, 39–45.

Willis, J. (2006). *Research-based strategies to ignite student learning: Insights from a neurologist and classroom teacher.* Alexandria, VA: ASCD.

Zajonc, R. B. (1968). Attitudinal effects of mere exposure. *Journal of Personality and Social Psychology, 9*, Monograph Supplement, No. 2, Part 2.

Zajonc, R. B. (1970). Brainwash: Familiarity breeds comfort. *Psychology Today*, (February), 32–35, 60–62.

Zajonc, R. B. (2001). Mere exposure: A gateway to the subliminal. *Current Directions in Psychological Science, 10*, 224–228.

Quote Reflections

Review the sidebar quotes contained in this chapter and select two that were especially meaningful or inspirational to you.

For each quote, provide a three- to five-sentence explanation why you chose it.

Reality Bite

Hate Crime: A Racially Motivated Murder

Jasper County, Texas, has a population of approximately 31,000 people. In this county, 80% of the people are White, 18% are Black, and 2% are of other races. The county's poverty rate is considerably higher than the national average, and its average household income is significantly lower. In 1998, the mayor, the president of the Chamber of Commerce, and two councilmen were Black. From the outside, Jasper appeared to be a town with racial harmony, and its Black and White leaders were quick to state that there was no racial tension in Jasper.

However, one day, James Byrd Jr.—a 49-year-old African American man—was walking home along a road one evening and was offered a ride by three White males. Rather than taking Byrd home, Lawrence Brewer (age 31), John King (age 23), and Shawn Berry (age 23), three men linked to White-supremacist groups, took Byrd to an isolated area and began beating him. They then dropped his pants to his ankles, painted his face black, chained Byrd to their truck, and dragged him for approximately three miles. The truck was driven in a zigzag fashion to inflict maximum pain on the victim. Byrd was decapitated after his body collided with a culvert in a ditch alongside the road. His skin, arms, genitalia, and other body parts were strewn along the road, while his torso was found dumped in front of a Black cemetery. Medical examiners testified that Byrd was alive for much of the dragging incident.

When they were brought to trial, the bodies of Brewer and King were covered with racist tattoos; they were eventually sentenced to death. As a result of the murder, Byrd's family created the James Byrd Foundation for Racial Healing. A wrought iron fence that separated Black and White graves for more than 150 years in Jasper Cemetery was removed in a special unity service. Members of the racist Ku Klux Klan have since visited the gravesite of Byrd several times, leaving racist stickers and other marks that angered the Jasper community and Byrd's family.

Source: *Louisiana Weekly* (February 3, 2003).

Reflection Questions

1. What factors do you think were responsible for this incident?

2. Could this incident have been prevented? If yes, how? If no, why not?

3. How likely do you think an incident like this could take place in your hometown or near your college campus?

4. If this event happened to take place in your hometown, how do you think members of your community would react?

Gaining Awareness of Your Group Identities

We are members of multiple groups at the same time and our membership in these overlapping groups can influence our personal development and identity. In the following figure, consider the shaded center circle to be yourself and the six unshaded circles to be six different groups you belong to and have influenced your development.

Fill in the unshaded circles with the names of groups to which you think you belong that have had the most influence on your personal development and identity. You can use the diversity spectrum (p. 234) to help you identify different groups to which you may be a member. Don't feel you have to fill in all six circles. What's more important is to identify those groups that you think have had a significant influence on your personal development or identity.

Reflection Questions

1. Which one of your groups has had the greatest influence on your personal development or identity? Why?

2. Have you ever felt limited or disadvantaged by being a member of any group(s) to which you belong? Why?

3. Have you ever felt advantaged or privileged by your membership in any group(s)? Why?

Intercultural Interview

1. Identify a person on your campus who is a member of an ethnic or racial group that you've had little previous contact. Ask that person for an interview, and during the interview, include the following questions:
   - What does "diversity" mean to you?
   - What prior experiences have affected your current viewpoints or attitudes about diversity?
   - What would you say have been the major influences and turning points in your life?
   - Who would you cite as your positive role models, heroes, or sources of inspiration?
   - What societal contributions made by your ethnic or racial group would you like others to be aware of and acknowledge?
   - What do you hope will never again be said about your ethnic or racial group?

2. If you were the interviewee instead of the interviewer, how would you have answered the above questions?

3. What do you think accounts for the differences (and similarities) between your answers to the above questions and those provided by the person you interviewed?

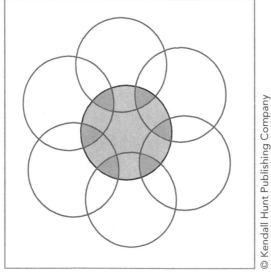

Hidden Bias Test

Go to www.tolerance.org/activity/test-yourself-hidden-bias and take one or more of the hidden bias tests on this website. These tests assess subtle bias with respect to gender, age, ethnic minority groups, religious denominations, sexual orientations, disabilities, and body weight.

After completing the test, answer the following questions:

1. Did the results reveal any bias(es) you weren't unaware of?

2. Did you think the assessment results were accurate or valid?

3. What do you think best accounts for or explains your results?

4. If your closest family member and best friend took the test, how do you think their results would compare with yours?

NOTES

What Majors Best Complement My Values and Personality?

Learning Objectives

Read to answer these key questions:

- What values are important to me?

- How does my personality align with my major and career interests?

- How can I utilize what I know about my values and personality to make decisions about my future?

Using Values to Make Important Life Decisions

Values are what we think is important and what we feel is right and good. Our values tell the world who we are. They help us to determine which goals are more valuable than others and to spend time on what is most important. Our values make us different and unique individuals. We often take pride in our values by displaying them on bumper stickers, tee shirts, and tattoos.

Values come from many sources, including our parents, friends, the media, our religious background, our culture, society, and the historical time in which we live. Knowing our values helps to make good decisions about work and life. For example, consider a situation in which a person is offered a high-paying job that involves a high degree of responsibility and stress. If the person values challenge and excitement and views stress as a motivator, the chances are that it would be a good decision to take the job. If the person values peace of mind and has a difficult time coping with stress, it might be better to forgo the higher income and maintain quality of life. Making decisions consistent with our values is one of the keys to happiness and success.

Researchers studied values in 70 different countries around the world and found 10 values rated as important around the world.[10] As you read the list, think about your own personal values.

The 10 Most Important Values around the World

- **Achievement**: personal success
- **Benevolence**: concern about the welfare of others
- **Conformity**: acting within social norms
- **Hedonism**: personal gratification and pleasure
- **Power**: status and prestige
- **Security**: safety, harmony, law, and order
- **Self-direction**: independent thought and action
- **Stimulation**: excitement, novelty, and challenge
- **Tradition**: respect for cultural or religious customs
- **Universalism**: understanding and appreciating all people and nature

---

Values Checklist

Assessing Your Personal Values

Use the following checklist to begin to think about what values are important to you.
Place a checkmark next to any value that is important to you. There are no right or wrong answers. If you
think of other values that are important to you, add them to the bottom of the list.

_____ Having financial security	_____ Having good family relationships
_____ Making a contribution to humankind	_____ Preserving the environment
_____ Being a good parent	_____ Having the respect of others
_____ Being honest	_____ Becoming famous
_____ Acquiring wealth	_____ Happiness
_____ Being a wise person	_____ Freedom and independence
_____ Becoming an educated person	_____ Common sense
_____ Believing in a higher power (God)	_____ Having pride in my culture
_____ Preserving civil rights	_____ Doing community service
_____ Never being bored	_____ Achieving my goals in life
_____ Enjoying life and having fun	_____ Having adventures
_____ Making something out of my life	_____ Having leisure time
_____ Being an ethical person	_____ Having good health
_____ Feeling safe and secure	_____ Being loyal
_____ Having a good marriage	_____ Having a sense of accomplishment
_____ Having good friends	_____ Participating in church activities
_____ Having social status	_____ Being physically fit
_____ Being patriotic	_____ Helping others
_____ Having power	_____ Being a good person
_____ Having good morals	_____ Having time to myself
_____ Being creative	_____ Loving and being loved
_____ Having control over my life	_____ Being physically attractive
_____ Growing and developing	_____ Achieving something important
_____ Feeling competent	_____ Accepting who I am
_____ Feeling relaxed	_____ Appreciating natural beauty
_____ Having prestige	_____ Using my artistic talents
_____ Improving society	_____ Feeling good about myself
_____ Having good mental health	_____ Making a difference

_____	Being a good athlete	_____	Other:	_____
_____	Enjoying the present moment	_____	Other:	_____
_____	Maintaining peace of mind	_____	Other:	_____

REFLECTION

What is your most important value? Why is it important to you?

QUIZ

Values

Test what you have learned by selecting the correct answers to the following questions.

1. Values are

    a. what we find interesting.
    b. what we find important.
    c. what we find entertaining.

2. Abraham Maslow described values as a

    a. circle.
    b. pyramid.
    c. square.

3. According to Maslow, our most basic needs are

    a. social.
    b. biological.
    c. intellectual.

4. According to Maslow, we are all aiming for

    a. independence.
    b. wealth.
    c. self-actualization.

5. Knowing what we value helps us to make good

    a. wages.
    b. decisions.
    c. expenditures.

REFLECTION

Write down your most important value. Write an intention statement about how you plan to act on this value. For example, my most important value is to maintain my good health. I intend to act on this value by eating right and exercising.

Interests

Test what you have learned by selecting the correct answers to the following questions.

1. Realistic people are likely to choose a career in

   a. construction or engineering.
   b. accounting or real estate.
   c. financial investments or banking.

2. Investigative people are likely to choose a career in

   a. art or music.
   b. teaching or social work.
   c. science or laboratory work.

3. Enterprising people are likely to choose a career in

   a. computer programming or accounting.
   b. business management or government.
   c. health care or social services.

4. Conventional people are likely to choose a career in

   a. health care or social services.
   b. financial investments or banking.
   c. manufacturing or transportation.

5. Social types generally

   a. enjoy working with tools and machines.
   b. are humanistic and idealistic.
   c. have skills in selling and communication.

Notes

1. U.S. Department of Labor, "O*Net Interest Profiler," available at http://onetcenter.org

2. U.S. Department of Labor, "O*Net Interest Profiler User's Guide," available at http://onetcenter.org

3. John L. Holland, *Making Vocational Choices: A Theory of Vocational Personalities and Work Environments* (2nd Ed.), (Englewood Cliffs, NJ: Prentice-Hall, 1985).

4. U.S. Department of Labor, "O*Net Interest Profiler User's Guide."

5. Adapted from U.S. Department of Labor, "O*Net Interest Profiler."

6. Job titles in this section from http://www.onetonline.org/find/descriptor/browse/Interests/

7. The Lifestyle Triangle adapted with permission from NTL Institute, "Urban Middle-Class Lifestyles in Transition," by Paula Jean Miller and Gideon Sjoberg, *Journal of Applied Behavioral Science* 9 (1973), nos. 2/3: 149.

To assure your success in college, it is important to choose the major that is best for you. If you choose a major and career that match your personality, interests, aptitudes, and values, you will enjoy your studies and excel in your work. It was Picasso who said that you know you enjoy your work when you do not notice the time passing by. If you can become interested in your work and studies, you are on your way to developing passion and joy in your life. If you can get up each morning and enjoy the work that you do (at least on most days), you will surely have one of the keys to happiness.

Choose a Major That Matches Your Gifts and Talents

The first step in choosing the major that is right for you is to understand your personality type. Psychologists have developed useful theories of personality that can help you understand how personality type relates to the choice of major and career. The personality theory used in this textbook is derived from the work of Swiss psychologist Carl Jung (1875–1961). Jung believed that we are born with a predisposition for certain personality preferences and that healthy development is based on the lifelong nurturing of inborn preferences rather than trying to change a person to become something different. Each personality type has gifts and talents that can be nurtured over a lifetime.

While assessments are not exact predictors of your future major and career, they provide useful information that will get you started on the path of career exploration and finding the college major that is best suited to you. Knowledge of your personality and the personalities of others is not only valuable in understanding yourself, but also in appreciating how others are different. This understanding of self and others will empower you to communicate and work effectively with others. Complete the AchieveWORKS Personality assessment that is included with this textbook before you begin this chapter. (See the inside front cover for further information.)

© Andril Kondiuk/Shutterstock.com

Understanding Personality Types

Just as no two fingerprints or snowflakes are exactly alike, each person is a different and unique individual. Even with this uniqueness, however, we can make some general statements about personality. When we make generalizations, we are talking about averages. These averages can provide useful information about ourselves and other people, but it is important to remember that no individual is exactly described by the average. As you read through the following descriptions of personality types, keep in mind that we are talking about generalizations or beginning points for discussion and thoughtful analysis.

As you read through your personality description from the AchieveWORKS Personality assessment and the information in this text, **focus on your personal strengths and talents**. Building on these personal strengths has several important benefits. It increases self-esteem and self-confidence, which contribute to your success and enjoyment of life. Building on your strengths provides the energy and motivation required to put in the effort needed to accomplish any worthwhile task. The assessment also identifies some of your possible weaknesses or "blind spots." Just be aware of these blind spots so that they do not interfere with your success. Being aware of your blind spots can even be used to your advantage. For example, some personality types thrive by working with people. A career that involves much public contact is a good match for this personality type, whereas choosing a career where public contact is limited can lead to job dissatisfaction. Knowing about your personality type can help you make the right decisions to maximize your potential.

Personality type has four dimensions:

1. Extraversion or Introversion

2. Sensing or Intuition

3. Thinking or Feeling

4. Judging or Perceiving

These dimensions of personality will be defined and examined in more depth in the sections that follow.

Extraversion or Introversion

The dimension of extraversion or introversion defines how we interact with the world and how our energy flows. In the general school population, 75 percent of students are usually extraverts and 25 percent are introverts.

Extraverts (E) focus their energy on the world outside themselves. They enjoy interaction with others and get to know a lot of different people. They enjoy and are usually good at communication. They are energized by social interaction and prefer being active. These types are often described as talkative and social.

Introverts (I) focus their energy on the world inside of themselves. They enjoy spending time alone to think about the world in order to understand it. Introverts prefer more limited social contacts, choosing smaller groups or one-on-one relationships. These types are often described as quiet or reserved.

We all use the introvert and extravert modes while functioning in our daily lives. Whether a person is an extravert or an introvert is a matter of preference, like being left- or right-handed. We can use our nondominant hand, but it is not as comfortable as using our dominant hand. We are usually more skillful in using the dominant hand. For example, introverts can learn to function well in social situations, but later may need some peace and quiet to recharge. On the other hand, social contact energizes the extravert.

One personality type is not better than the other: it is just different. Being an extravert is not better than being an introvert. Each type has unique gifts and talents that can be used in different occupations. An extravert might enjoy working in an occupation with lots of public contact, such as being a receptionist or handling public relations. An introvert might enjoy being an accountant or writer. However, as with all of the personality dimensions, a person may have traits of both types.

Introverts and Extraverts

The list below describes some qualities of introverts and extraverts. **For each pair of items**, quickly choose the phrase that describes you best and highlight or place a checkmark next to it. Remember that one type is not better than another. You may also find that you are a combination type and act like an introvert in some situations and an extravert in others. Each type has gifts and talents that can be used in choosing the best major and career for you. To get an estimate of your preference, notice which column has the most checkmarks.

Introvert (I)	Extravert (E)
_____ Energized by having quiet time alone	_____ Energized by social interaction
_____ Tend to think first and talk later	_____ Tend to talk first and think later
_____ Tend to think things through quietly	_____ Tend to think out loud
_____ Tend to respond slowly, after thinking	_____ Tend to respond quickly, before thinking
_____ Avoid being the center of attention	_____ Like to be the center of attention
_____ Difficult to get to know, private	_____ Easy to get to know, outgoing
_____ Have a few close friends	_____ Have many friends, know lots of people
_____ Prefer quiet for concentration	_____ Can read or talk with background noise
_____ Listen more than talk	_____ Talk more than listen
_____ View telephone calls as a distraction	_____ View telephone calls as a welcome break
_____ Talk to a few people at parties	_____ Talk to many different people at parties
_____ Share special occasions with one or a few people	_____ Share special occasions with large groups
_____ Prefer to study alone	_____ Prefer to study with others in a group
_____ Prefer the library to be quiet	_____ Talk with others in the library
_____ Described as quiet or reserved	_____ Described as talkative or friendly
_____ Work systematically	_____ Work through trial and error

Here are some qualities that describe the ideal work environment. Again, as you **read through each pair of items**, place a checkmark next to the work environment that you prefer.

Introvert (I)	Extravert (E)
_____ Work alone or with individuals	_____ Much public contact
_____ Quiet for concentration	_____ High-energy environment
_____ Communication one-on-one	_____ Present ideas to a group
_____ Work in small groups	_____ Work as part of a team
_____ Focus on one project until complete	_____ Variety and action
_____ Work without interruption	_____ Talk to others
_____ **Total** (from both charts above)	_____ **Total** (from both charts above)

Do these results agree with your personality assessment on the AchieveWORKS Personality assessment? If your results are the same, this is a good indication that your results are useful and accurate. Are there some differences with the results obtained from your personality assessment? If your results are different, this provides an opportunity for further reflection about your personality type. Here are a couple of reasons why your results may be different.

1. You may be a combination type with varying degrees of preference for each type.

2. You may have chosen your personality type on the AchieveWORKS Personality assessment based on what you think is best rather than what you truly are. Students sometimes do this because of the myth that there are good and bad personality types. It is important to remember that each personality type has strengths and weaknesses. By identifying strengths, you can build on them by choosing the right major and career. By being aware of weaknesses, you can come up with strategies to compensate for them to be successful.

Look at the total number of checkmarks for extravert and introvert on the two above charts. Do you lean toward being an introvert or an extravert? Remember that one type is not better than the other and each has unique gifts and talents. On the chart below, place an X on the line to indicate how much you prefer introversion or extraversion. If you selected most of the introvert traits, place your X somewhere on the left side. If you selected most of the extravert traits, place your X somewhere on the right side. If you are equally introverted and extraverted, place your X in the middle.

Introvert _____|_____ Extravert

Do you generally prefer introversion or extraversion? In the box below, write **I** for introversion or **E** for extraversion. If there is a tie between **E** and **I**, write **I**.

☐

Notice that it is possible to be a combination type. At times you might prefer to act like an introvert, and at other times you might prefer to act like an extravert. It is beneficial to be able to balance these traits. However, for combination types, it is more difficult to select specific occupations that match this type

REFLECTION

Look at the results from AchieveWORKS Personality assessment and your own self-assessment above. Are you an introvert or an extravert or a combination of these two types? Can you give examples of how it affects your social life, school, or work? Write a paragraph about this preference.

Sensing or Intuition

The dimension of sensing or intuition describes how we take in information. In the general school population, 70 percent of students are usually sensing types and 30 percent are intuitive types.

Sensing (S) persons prefer to use the senses to take in information (what they see, hear, taste, touch, smell). They focus on "what is" and trust information that is concrete and observable. They learn through experience.

Intuitive (N) persons rely on instincts and focus on "what could be." While we all use our five senses to perceive the world, intuitive people are interested in relationships, possibilities, meanings, and implications. They value inspiration and trust their "sixth sense" or hunches. (Intuitive is designated as N so it is not confused with I for Introvert.)

We all use both of these modes in our daily lives, but we usually have a preference for one mode or the other. Again, there is no best preference. Each type has special skills that can be applied to the job market. For example, you would probably want your tax preparer to be a sensing type who focuses on concrete information and fills out your tax form correctly. An inventor or artist would probably be an intuitive type.

ACTIVITY

Sensing and Intuitive

Here are some qualities of sensing and intuitive persons. As you **read through each pair of items**, quickly highlight or place a checkmark next to the item that usually describes yourself.

Sensing (S)	INtuitive (N)
_____ Trust what is certain and concrete	_____ Trust inspiration and inference
_____ Prefer specific answers to questions	_____ Prefer general answers that leave room for interpretation
_____ Like new ideas if they have practical applications (if you can use them)	_____ Like new ideas for their own sake (you don't need a practical use for them)
_____ Value realism and common sense	_____ Value imagination and innovation
_____ Think about things one at a time and step by step	_____ Think about many ideas at once as they come to you
_____ Like to improve and use skills learned before	_____ Like to learn new skills and get bored using the same skills
_____ More focused on the present	_____ More focused on the future
_____ Concentrate on what you are doing	_____ Wonder what is next
_____ Do something	_____ Think about doing something
_____ See tangible results	_____ Focus on possibilities
_____ If it isn't broken, don't fix it	_____ There is always a better way to do it

Sensing (S)	INtuitive (N)
_____ Prefer working with facts and figures	_____ Prefer working with ideas and theories
_____ Focus on reality	_____ Use fantasy
_____ Seeing is believing	_____ Anything is possible
_____ Tend to be specific and literal (say what you mean)	_____ Tend to be general and figurative (use comparisons and analogies)
_____ See what is here and now	_____ See the big picture

Here are some qualities that describe the ideal work environment. Again, as you **read through each pair of items**, place a checkmark next to the work environment that you prefer.

Sensing (S)	INtuitive (N)
_____ Use and practice skills	_____ Learn new skills
_____ Work with known facts	_____ Explore new ideas and approaches
_____ See measurable results	_____ Work with theories
_____ Focus on practical benefits	_____ Use imagination and be original
_____ Learn through experience	_____ Freedom to follow your inspiration
_____ Pleasant environment	_____ Challenging environment
_____ Use standard procedures	_____ Invent new products and procedures
_____ Work step-by-step	_____ Work in bursts of energy
_____ Do accurate work	_____ Find creative solutions
_____ **Total** (from both charts above)	_____ **Total** (from both charts above)

Look at the two charts above and see whether you tend to be more sensing or intuitive. One preference is not better than another: it is just different. On the chart below, place an X on the line to indicate your preference for sensing or intuitive. Again, notice that it is possible to be a combination type with both sensing and intuitive preferences.

Sensing _____|_____Intuitive

Do you generally prefer sensing or intuition? In the box below, write **S** for sensing or **N** for intuitive. If there is a tie between **S** and **N**, write **N**.

```
┌─────┐
│     │
│     │
└─────┘
```

REFLECTION

Look at the results from AchieveWORKS Personality assessment and your own self-assessment above. Are you a sensing, intuitive, or combination type? Can you give examples of how it affects your social life, school, or work? Write a paragraph about this preference.

Thinking or Feeling

The dimension of thinking or feeling defines how we prefer to make decisions. In the general school population, 60 percent of males are thinking types and 40 percent are feeling types. For females, 60 percent are feeling types and 40 percent are thinking types.

Thinking (T) individuals make decisions based on logic. They are objective and analytical. They look at all the evidence and reach an impersonal conclusion. They are concerned with what they think is right.

Feeling (F) individuals make decisions based on what is important to them and matches their personal values. They are concerned about what they feel is right.

We all use logic and have feelings and emotions that play a part in decision making. However, the thinking person prefers to make decisions based on logic, and the feeling person prefers to make decisions according to what is important to self and others. This is one category in which men and women often differ. Most women are feeling types, and most men are logical types. When men and women are arguing, you might hear the following:

Man: "I think that . . ."

Woman: "I feel that . . ."

By understanding these differences, it is possible to improve communication and understanding. Be careful with generalizations, since 40 percent of men and women would not fit this pattern.

When thinking about careers, a thinking type would make a good judge or computer programmer. A feeling type would probably make a good social worker or kindergarten teacher.

ACTIVITY

Thinking and Feeling

The following chart shows some qualities of thinking and feeling types. As you **read through each pair of items**, quickly highlight or place a checkmark next to the items that usually describe yourself.

Thinking (T)	Feeling (F)
_____ Apply impersonal analysis to problems	_____ Consider the effect on others
_____ Value logic and justice	_____ Value empathy and harmony
_____ Fairness is important	_____ There are exceptions to every rule
_____ Truth is more important than tact	_____ Tact is more important than truth
_____ Motivated by achievement and accomplishment	_____ Motivated by being appreciated by others
_____ Feelings are valid if they are logical	_____ Feelings are valid whether they make sense or not
_____ Good decisions are logical	_____ Good decisions take others' feelings into account

Thinking (T)	Feeling (F)
_____ Described as cool, calm, and objective	_____ Described as caring and emotional
_____ Love can be analyzed	_____ Love cannot be analyzed
_____ Firm-minded	_____ Gentle-hearted
_____ More important to be right	_____ More important to be liked
_____ Remember numbers and figures	_____ Remember faces and names
_____ Prefer clarity	_____ Prefer harmony
_____ Find flaws and critique	_____ Look for the good and compliment
_____ Prefer firmness	_____ Prefer persuasion

Here are some qualities that describe the ideal work environment. As you **read through each pair of items**, place a checkmark next to the items that usually describe the work environment that you prefer.

Thinking (T)	Feeling (F)
_____ Maintain business environment	_____ Maintain close personal relationships
_____ Work with people I respect	_____ Work in a friendly, relaxed environment
_____ Be treated fairly	_____ Be able to express personal values
_____ Fair evaluations	_____ Appreciation for good work
_____ Solve problems	_____ Make a personal contribution
_____ Challenging work	_____ Harmonious work situation
_____ Use logic and analysis	_____ Help others
_____ **Total** (from both charts above)	_____ **Total** (from both charts above)

While we all use thinking and feeling, what is your preferred type? Look at the charts above and notice whether you are more the thinking or feeling type. One is not better than the other. On the chart below, place an X on the line to indicate how much you prefer thinking or feeling.

Thinking _____|_____ Feeling

Do you generally prefer thinking or feeling? In the box below, write **T** for thinking or **F** for feeling. If there is a tie between **T** and **F**, write **F**.

```
┌──────┐
│      │
│      │
└──────┘
```

REFLECTION

Look at the results from AchieveWORKS Personality assessment and your own self-assessment above. Are you a thinking, feeling, or combination type? Can you give examples of how it affects your social life, school, or work? Write a paragraph about this preference.

Judging or Perceiving

The dimension of judging or perceiving refers to how we deal with the external world. In other words, do we prefer the world to be structured or unstructured? In the general school population, the percentage of each of these types is approximately equal.

Judging (J) types like to live in a structured, orderly, and planned way. They are happy when their lives are structured and matters are settled. They like to have control over their lives. **Judging does not mean to judge others.** Think of this type as being orderly and organized.

Perceptive (P) types like to live in a spontaneous and flexible way. They are happy when their lives are open to possibilities. They try to understand life rather than control it. **Think of this type as spontaneous and flexible.**

Since these types have very opposite ways of looking at the world, there is a great deal of potential for conflict between them unless there is an appreciation for the gifts and talents of both. In any situation, we can benefit from people who represent these very different points of view. For example, in a business situation, the judging type would be good at managing the money, while the perceptive type would be good at helping the business to adapt to a changing marketplace. It is good to be open to all the possibilities and to be flexible, as well as to have some structure and organization.

ACTIVITY

Judging and Perceptive

As you **read through each pair of items**, quickly highlight or place a checkmark next to the items that generally describe yourself.

Judging (J)	Perceptive (P)
_____ Happy when the decisions are made and finished	_____ Happy when the options are left open; something better may come along
_____ Work first, play later	_____ Play first, do the work later
_____ It is important to be on time	_____ Time is relative
_____ Time flies	_____ Time is elastic
_____ Feel comfortable with routine	_____ Dislike routine
_____ Generally keep things in order	_____ Prefer creative disorder
_____ Set goals and work toward them	_____ Change goals as new opportunities arise
_____ Emphasize completing the task	_____ Emphasize how the task is done
_____ Like to finish projects	_____ Like to start projects
_____ Meet deadlines	_____ What deadline?
_____ Like to know what I am getting into	_____ Like new possibilities and situations
_____ Relax when things are organized	_____ Relax when necessary
_____ Follow a routine	_____ Explore the unknown
_____ Focused	_____ Easily distracted
_____ Work steadily	_____ Work in spurts of energy

Here are some qualities that describe the ideal work environment. Again, as you **read through each pair of items**, place a checkmark next to the work environment that you prefer.

Judging (J)		Perceptive (P)	
_____	Follow a schedule	_____	Be spontaneous
_____	Clear directions	_____	Minimal rules and structure
_____	Organized work	_____	Flexibility
_____	Logical order	_____	Many changes
_____	Control my job	_____	Respond to emergencies
_____	Stability and security	_____	Take risks and be adventurous
_____	Work on one project until done	_____	Juggle many projects
_____	Steady work	_____	Variety and action
_____	Satisfying work	_____	Fun and excitement
_____	Like having high responsibility	_____	Like having interesting work
_____	Accomplish goals on time	_____	Work at my own pace
_____	Clear and concrete assignments	_____	Minimal supervision
_____	**Total** (from both charts above)	_____	**Total** (from both charts above)

Look at the charts above and notice whether you are more the judging type (orderly and organized) or the perceptive type (spontaneous and flexible). We need the qualities of both types to be successful and deal with the rapid changes in today's world. On the chart below, place an X on the line to indicate how much you prefer judging or perceiving.

Judging _____|_____ Perceptive

Do you generally have judging or perceptive traits? In the box below, write **J** for judging or **P** for perceptive. If there is a tie between **J** and **P**, write **P**.

REFLECTION

Look at the results from AchieveWORKS Personality assessment and your own self-assessment above. Are you a thinking, feeling, or combination type? Can you give examples of how it affects your social life, school, or work? Write a paragraph about this preference.

"Knowing thyself is the height of wisdom."
Socrates

Summarize Your Results

Look at your results above and summarize them on this composite chart. Notice that we are all unique, according to where the Xs fall on the scale.

Extravert (E) _____ Introvert (I)

Sensing (S) _____ Intuitive (N)

Thinking (T) _____ Feeling (F)

Judging (J) _____ Perceptive (P)

Write the letters representing each of your preferences: _____

The above letters represent your estimated personality type based on your understanding and knowledge of self. It is a good idea to confirm that this type is correct for you by completing the online AchieveWORKS Personality assessment.

© Gustavo Frazao/Shutterstock.com

Personality Types

Test what you have learned by selecting the correct answer to the following questions.

1. A person who is energized by social interaction is a/an:

   a. introvert
   b. extravert
   c. feeling type

2. A person who is quiet and reserved is a/an:

   a. introvert
   b. extravert
   c. perceptive type

3. A person who relies on experience and trusts information that is concrete and observable is a/an:

   a. judging type
   b. sensing type
   c. perceptive type

4. A person who focuses on "what could be" is a/an:

   a. perceptive type
   b. thinking type
   c. intuitive type

5. A person who makes decisions based on logic is a/an:

   a. thinker
   b. perceiver
   c. sensor

6. A person who makes decisions based on personal values is a/an:

   a. feeling type
   b. thinking type
   c. judging type

7. The perceptive type:

   a. has extrasensory perception
   b. likes to live life in a spontaneous and flexible way
   c. always considers feelings before making a decision

8. The judging type likes to:

   a. judge others
   b. use logic
   c. live in a structured and orderly way

9. Personality assessments are an exact predictor of your best major and career.

   a. true
   b. false

10. Some personality types are better than others.

   a. true
   b. false

Personality and Career Choice

While it is not possible to predict exactly your career and college major by knowing your personality type, it can help provide opportunities for exploration. The AchieveWORKS personality assessment links your personality type with suggested matching careers in the O*Net career database continually updated by the U.S. Department of Labor. You can find additional information at the College Success 1 website: http://www.collegesuccess1.com/careers.html. This page includes a description of each type, general occupations to consider, specific job titles, and suggested college majors.

© iQoncept/Shutterstock.com

Personality and Preferred Work Environment

Knowing your personality type will help you to understand your preferred work environment and provide some insights into selecting the major and career that you would enjoy. Selecting the work environment that matches your personal preferences helps you to be energized on the job and to minimize stress. Understanding other types will help you to work effectively with co-workers. As you read this section, think about your ideal work environment and how others are different.

Extraverts are career generalists who use their skills in a variety of ways. They like variety and action in a work environment that provides the opportunity for social interaction. Extraverts communicate well and meet people easily. They like to talk while working and are interested in other people and what they are doing. They enjoy variety on the job and like to perform their work in different settings. They learn new tasks by talking with others and trying out new ideas. Extraverts are energized by working as part of a team, leading others in achieving goals, and having opportunities to communicate with others.

Introverts are career specialists who develop in-depth skills. The introvert likes quiet for concentration and likes to focus on a work task until it is completed. They need time to think before taking action. This type often chooses to work alone or with one other person and prefers written communication such as emails to oral communication or presentations. They learn new tasks by reading and reflecting and using mental practice. Introverts are energized when they can work in a quiet environment with few interruptions. They are stressed when they have to work in a noisy environment and do not have time alone to concentrate on a project.

The **sensing** type is realistic and practical and likes to develop standard ways of doing the job and following a routine. They are observant and interested in facts and finding the truth. They keep accurate track of details, make lists, and are good at doing precise work. This type learns from personal experience and the experience of others. They use their experience to move up the job ladder. Sensing types are energized when they are doing practical work with tangible outcomes where they are required to organize facts and details, use common sense, and focus on one project at a time. They are stressed when they have to deal with frequent or unexpected change.

The **intuitive** type likes to work on challenging and complex problems where they can follow their inspirations to find creative solutions. They like change and finding new ways of doing work. This type focuses on the whole picture rather than the details. The intuitive type is an initiator, promoter, and inventor of ideas. They enjoy learning a new skill more than using it. They often change careers to follow their creative inspirations. Intuitive types are energized by working in an environment where they can use creative insight, imagination, originality, and individual initiative. They are stressed when they have to deal with too many details or have little opportunity for creativity.

The **thinking** type likes to use logical analysis in making decisions. They are objective and rational and treat others fairly. They want logical reasons before accepting any new ideas. They follow policy and are often firm-minded and critical, especially when dealing with illogic in others. They easily learn facts, theories, and principles. They are interested in careers with money, prestige, or influence. Thinking types are energized when they are respected for their expertise and recognized for a job well done. They enjoy working with others who are competent and efficient. They become stressed when they work with people they consider to be illogical, unfair, incompetent, or overly emotional.

© cristovao/Shutterstock.com

The **feeling** type likes harmony and the support of co-workers. They are personal, enjoy warm relationships, and relate well to most people. Feeling types know their personal values and apply them consistently. They enjoy doing work that provides a service to people and often do work that requires them to understand and analyze their own emotions and those of others. They prefer a friendly work environment and like to learn with others. They enjoy careers in which they can make a contribution to humanity. Feeling types are energized by working in a friendly, congenial, and supportive work environment. They are stressed when there is conflict in the work environment, especially when working with controlling or demanding people.

The **judging** type likes a work environment that is structured, settled, and organized. They prefer work assignments that are clear and definite. The judging type makes lists and plans to get the job done on time. They make quick decisions and like to have the work finished. They are good at doing purposeful and exacting work. They prefer to learn only the essentials that are necessary to do the job. This type carefully plans their career path. Judging types are energized by working in a predictable and orderly environment with clear responsibilities and deadlines. They become stressed when the work environment becomes disorganized or unpredictable.

> "True greatness is starting where you are, using what you have, and doing what you can."
>
> Arthur Ashe

The **perceptive** type likes to be spontaneous and go with the flow. They are comfortable in handling the unplanned or unexpected in the work environment. They prefer to be flexible in their work and feel restricted by structures and schedules. They are good at handling work which requires change and adaptation. They are tolerant and have a "live and let live" attitude toward others. Decisions are often postponed because this type wants to know all there is to know and explore all the options before making a decision. This type is often a career changer who takes advantage of new job openings and opportunities for change. Perceptive types are energized when the work environment is flexible and they can relax and control their own time. They are stressed when they have to meet deadlines or work under excessive rules and regulations.

More on Personality Type

Personality and Decision Making

Your personality type affects how you think and how you make decisions. Knowing your decision-making style will help you make good decisions about your career and personal life as well as work with others in creative problem solving. Each

© Stephen Coburn/Shutterstock. com

personality type views the decision-making process in a different way. Ideally, a variety of types would be involved in making a decision so that the strengths of each type could be utilized. As you read through the following descriptions, think about your personality type and how you make decisions as well as how others are different.

The **introvert** thinks up ideas and reflects on the problem before acting. The **extravert** acts as the communicator in the decision-making process. Once the decision is made, they take action and implement the decision. The **intuitive** type develops theories and uses intuition to come up with ingenious solutions to the problem. The **sensing** type applies personal experience to the decision-making process and focuses on solutions that are practical and realistic.

The thinking and feeling dimensions of personality are the most important factors in determining how a decision is made. Of course, people use both thinking and feeling in the decision-making process, but tend to prefer or trust either thinking or feeling. Those who prefer **thinking** use cause-and-effect reasoning and solve problems with logic. They use objective and impersonal criteria and include all the consequences of alternative solutions in the decision-making process. They are interested in finding out what is true and what is false. They use laws and principles to treat everyone fairly. Once a decision is made, they are firm-minded, since the decision was based on logic. This type is often critical of those who do not use logic in the decision-making process. The **feeling** type considers human values and motives in the decision-making process (whether they are logical or not) and values harmony and maintaining good relationships. They consider carefully how much they care about each of the alternatives and how they will affect other people. They are interested in making a decision that is agreeable to all parties. Feeling types are tactful and skillful in dealing with people.

It is often asked if thinking types have feelings. They do have feelings, but use them as a criterion to be factored into the decision-making process. Thinking types are more comfortable when feelings are controlled and often think that feeling types are too emotional. Thinking types may have difficulties when they apply logic in a situation where a feeling response is needed, such as in dealing with a spouse. Thinking types need to know that people are important in making decisions. Feeling types need to know that behavior will have logical consequences and that they may need to keep emotions more controlled to work effectively with thinking types.

Judging and **perceptive** types have opposite decision-making strategies. The judging type is very methodical and cautious in making decisions. Once they have gone through the decision-making steps, they like to make decisions quickly so that they can have closure and finish the project. The perceptive type is an adventurer who wants to look at all the possibilities before making a decision. They are open-minded and curious and often resist closure to look at more options.

If a combination of types collaborates on a decision, it is more likely that the decision will be a good one that takes into account creative possibilities, practicality, logical consequences, and human values.

Personality and Time Management

How we manage our time is not just a result of personal habits: it is also a reflection of our personality type. Probably the dimension of personality type most connected to time management is the judging or perceptive trait. **Judging** types like to have things under control and live in a planned and orderly manner. **Perceptive** types prefer more spontaneity and flexibility. Understanding the differences between these two types will help you to better understand yourself and others.

Judging types are naturally good at time management. They often use schedules as a tool for time management and organization. Judging types plan their time and work steadily to accomplish goals. They are good at meeting deadlines and often put off relaxation, recreation, and fun. They relax after projects are completed. If they have too many projects, they find it difficult to find time for recreation. Since judging types like to have projects under control, there is a danger that projects will be completed too quickly and that quality will suffer. Judging types may need to slow down and take the time to do quality work. They may also need to make relaxation and recreation a priority.

Perceptive types are more open-ended and prefer to be spontaneous. They take time to relax, have fun, and participate in recreation. In working on a project, perceptive types want to brainstorm all the possibilities and are not too concerned about finishing projects. This type procrastinates when the time comes to make a final decision and finish a project. There is always more information to gather and more possibilities to explore. Perceptive types are easily distracted and may move from project to project. They may have several jobs going at once. These types need to try to focus on a few projects at a time in order to complete them. Perceptive types need to work on becoming more organized so that projects can be completed on time.

Research has shown that students who are judging types are more likely to have a higher grade point average in the first semester.[1] It has also been found that the greater the preference for intuition, introversion, and judgment, the better the grade point average.[2] Why is this true? Many college professors are intuitive types that use intuition and creative ideas. The college environment requires quiet time for reading and studying, which is one of the preferences of introverts. Academic environments require structure, organization, and completion of assignments. To be successful in an academic environment requires adaptation by some personality types. Extroverts need to spend more quiet time reading and studying. Sensing types need to gain an understanding of intuitive types. Perceptive types need to use organization to complete assignments on time.

© STILLFX/Shutterstock.com

Personality and Money

Does your personality type affect how you deal with money? Otto Kroeger and Janet Thuesen make some interesting observations about how different personality types deal with money.

- **Judging types (orderly and organized).** These types excel at financial planning and money management. They file their tax forms early and pay their bills on time.

- **Perceptive types (spontaneous and flexible).** These types adapt to change and are more creative. Perceivers, especially intuitive perceivers, tend to freak out as the April 15 tax deadline approaches and as bills become due.

- **Feeling types (make decisions based on feelings).** These types are not very money-conscious. They believe that money should be used to serve humanity. They are often attracted to low-paying jobs that serve others.[3]

In studying stockbrokers, these same authors note that ISTJs (introvert, sensing, thinking, and judging types) are the most conservative investors, earning a small but reliable return on investments. The ESTPs (extravert, sensing, thinking, perceptive types) and ENTPs (extravert, intuitive, thinking, perceptive types) take the biggest risks and earn the greatest returns.[4]

Personality and Learning Strategies

Knowing about your personality type can help you to choose learning strategies that work for you.

© Monkey Business Images/Shutterstock.com

- **Extraverts** enjoy interactions with others and like to get to know other people. They learn best by discussing what they have learned with others. Form a study group. Be careful that excess socialization does not distract you from getting your studying done.

- **Introverts** are more quiet and reserved. They enjoy spending time alone to think about what they are studying. Study in the library. Be careful about missing out on the opportunities to share ideas with others.

- **Sensing** types focus on the senses (what they can see, hear, taste, touch, and smell.) These types are good at mastering the facts and details. Improve learning by first focusing on the big picture or broad outline and then the details will be easier to remember.

- **Intuitive** types focus on the big picture and may miss the details. Ask yourself, "What is the main point?" To improve learning, begin by looking at the big picture or broader outline and then organize the facts and details under the main ideas so you can recall them.

- **Thinking** types are good at logic. Make a personal connection with the material by asking yourself, "What do I think of these ideas?" Discuss or debate your ideas with others while remembering to respect their ideas.

- **Feeling** types are motivated by finding personal meaning in their studies. Ask yourself, "How is this material related to my life and what is important to me?" Look for a supportive environment or study group.

- **Judging** types are good at organizing the material to be learned and working steadily to accomplish their goals. Organize the material to be learned into manageable chunks to aid in recall.

- **Perceptive** types are spontaneous, flexible, adaptable, and open to new information. Pay attention to organizing your work and meeting deadlines to improve success in college and on the job. Be careful not to overextend yourself by working on too many projects at once.

Understanding Your Professor's Personality

© Alexander Raths/Shutterstock.com

Different personality types have different expectations of teachers.

- Extraverts want faculty who encourage class discussion.
- Introverts want faculty who give clear lectures.
- Sensing types want faculty who give clear and specific assignments.
- Intuitive types want faculty who encourage independent thinking.
- Thinking types want faculty who make logical presentations.
- Feeling types want faculty who establish personal rapport with students.
- Judging types want faculty to be organized.
- Perceptive types want faculty to be entertaining and inspiring.

College students and faculty often have different personality types. In summary,

College faculty tend to be	College students tend to be
Introverted	Extraverted
Intuitive	Sensing
Judging	Perceptive

Of course, the above is not always true, but there is a good probability that you will have college professors who are very different from you. What can you do if you and your professor have different personality types? First, try to understand the professor's personality. This has been called "psyching out the professor." You can usually tell the professor's personality type on the first day of class by examining class materials and observing his or her manner of presentation. If you understand the professor's personality type, you will know what to expect. Next, try to appreciate what the professor has to offer. You may need to adapt your expectations to be successful. For example, if you are an introvert, make an effort to participate in class discussions. If you are a perceptive type, be careful to meet the due dates of your assignments.

Personality and Career Choice

While it is not possible to predict exactly your career and college major by knowing your personality type, it can be helpful in providing opportunities for exploration. Here are some general descriptions of personality types and preferred careers. Included are general occupational fields, frequently chosen occupations, and suggested majors. These suggestions about career selections are based on the general characteristics of each type and research that correlates personality type with choice of a satisfying career.[5] Read the descriptions, careers and majors that match your personality type and then continue your career exploration with the online database in the Do What You Are personality assessment included with your textbook.

© 2014, iQoncept. Used under license with Shutterstock, Inc.

ISTJ

ISTJs are responsible, loyal, stable, practical, down-to-earth, hardworking, and reliable. They can be depended upon to follow through with tasks. They value tradition, family, and security. They are natural leaders who prefer to work alone, but can adapt to working with teams if needed. They like to be independent and have time to think things through. They are able to remember and use concrete facts and information. They make decisions by applying logic and rational thinking. They appreciate structured and orderly environments and deliver products and services in an efficient and orderly way.

General occupations to consider

business	education	health care
service	technical	military
law and law enforcement	engineering	management

Specific job titles

business executive	lawyer	electronic technician
administrator	judge	computer occupations
manager	police officer	dentist
real estate agent	detective	pharmacist
accountant	corrections officer	primary care physician
bank employee	teacher (math, trade,	nursing administrator
stockbroker	technical)	respiratory therapist
auditor	educational administrator	physical therapist
hairdresser	coach	optometrist
cosmetologist	engineer	chemist
legal secretary	electrician	military officer or enlistee

College majors

business	engineering	chemistry
education	computers	biology
mathematics	health occupations	vocational training
law		

From *Explorer's Guide: Starting Your College Journey with a Sense of Purpose*, Third Edition
by Bill Millard.

ISTP

ISTPs are independent, practical, and easygoing. They prefer to work individually and frequently like to work outdoors. These types like working with objects and often are good at working with their hands and mastering tools. They are interested in how and why things work and are able to apply technical knowledge to solving practical problems. Their logical thinking makes them good troubleshooters and problem solvers. They enjoy variety, new experiences, and taking risks. They prefer environments with little structure and have a talent for managing crises. The ISTP is happy with occupations that involve challenge, change, and variety.

General occupations to consider

sales	technical	business and finance
service	health care	vocational training
corrections		

Specific job titles

sales manager	engineer	office manager
insurance agent	electronics technician	small business manager
cook	software developer	banker
firefighter	computer programmer	economist
pilot	radiologic technician	legal secretary
race car driver	exercise physiologist	paralegal
police officer	coach	computer repair
corrections officer	athlete	airline mechanic
judge	dental assistant/hygienist	carpenter
attorney	physician	construction worker
intelligence agent	optometrist	farmer
detective	physical therapist	military officer or enlistee

College majors

business	computers	health occupations
vocational training	biology	physical education
law		

ISFJ

ISFJs are quiet, friendly, responsible, hardworking, productive, devoted, accurate, thorough, and careful. They value security, stability, and harmony. They like to focus on one person or project at a time. ISFJs prefer to work with individuals and are very skillful in understanding people and their needs. They often provide service to others in a very structured way. They are careful observers, remember facts, and work on projects requiring accuracy and attention to detail. They have a sense of space and function that leads to artistic endeavors such as interior decorating or landscaping. ISFJs are most comfortable working in environments that are orderly, structured, and traditional. While they often work quietly behind the scenes, they like their contributions to be recognized and appreciated.

General occupations to consider

health care	education	artistic
social service	business	religious occupations
corrections	technical	vocational training

Specific job titles

nurse	social worker	counselor
physician	social services	secretary
medical technologist	administrator	cashier
dental hygienist	child care worker	accountant
health education	speech pathologist	personnel administrator
practitioner	librarian	credit counselor
dietician	curator	business manager
physical therapist	genealogist	paralegal
nursing educator	corrections worker	computer occupations
health administrator	probation officer	engineer
medical secretary	teacher (preschool,	interior decorator
dentist	grades 1–12)	home economist
medical assistant	guidance counselor	religious educator
optometrist	educational administrator	clergy
occupational therapist		

College majors

health occupations	education	graphics
biology	business	religious studies
psychology	engineering	vocational training
sociology	art	

ISFP

ISFPs are quiet, reserved, trusting, loyal, committed, sensitive, kind, creative, and artistic. They have an appreciation for life and value serenity and aesthetic beauty. These types are individualistic and generally have no desire to lead or follow; they prefer to work independently. They have a keen awareness of their environment and often have a special bond with children and animals. ISFPs are service-oriented and like to help others. They like to be original and unconventional. They dislike rules and structure and need space and freedom to do things in their own way.

General occupations to consider

artists	technical	business
health care	service	vocational training

Specific job titles

artist	recreation services	forester
designer	physical therapist	botanist
fashion designer	radiologic technician	geologist
jeweler	medical assistant	mechanic
gardener	dental assistant/hygienist	marine biologist
potter	veterinary assistant	teacher (science, art)
painter	veterinarian	police officer
dancer	animal groomer/trainer	beautician
landscape designer	dietician	merchandise planner
carpenter	optician/optometrist	stock clerk
electrician	exercise physiologist	store keeper
engineer	occupational therapist	counselor
chef	art therapist	social worker
nurse	pharmacy technician	legal secretary
counselor	respiratory therapist	paralegal

College majors

art	forestry	psychology
health occupations	geology	counseling
engineering	education	social work
physical education	business	vocational training
biology		

INFJ

INFJs are idealistic, complex, compassionate, authentic, creative, and visionary. They have strong value systems and search for meaning and purpose to life. Because of their strong value systems, INFJs are natural leaders or at least follow those with similar ideas. They intuitively understand people and ideas and come up with new ideas to provide service to others. These types like to organize their time and be in control of their work.

General occupations to consider

counseling	religious occupations	health care
education	creative occupations	social services
science	arts	business

Specific job titles

career counselor	director of religious	dental hygienist
psychologist	education	speech pathologist
teacher (high school or	fine artist	nursing educator
college English, art,	playwright	medical secretary
music, social sciences,	novelist	pharmacist
drama, foreign	poet	occupational therapist
languages, health)	designer	human resources
librarian	architect	manager
home economist	art director	marketer
social worker	health care administrator	employee assistance
clergy	physician	program
	biologist	merchandise planner
		environmental lawyer

College majors

psychology	drama	architecture
counseling	foreign languages	biology
education	English	business
art	health occupations	law
music	social work	science

INFP

INFPs are loyal, devoted, sensitive, creative, inspirational, flexible, easygoing, complex, and authentic. They are original and individualistic and prefer to work alone or with other caring and supportive individuals. These types are service-oriented and interested in personal growth. They develop deep relationships because they understand people and are genuinely interested in them. They dislike dealing with details and routine work. They prefer a flexible working environment with a minimum of rules and regulations.

General occupations to consider

creative arts	counseling	health care
education	religious occupations	organizational development

Specific job titles

artist	photographer	dietician
designer	carpenter	psychiatrist
writer	teacher (art, drama,	physical therapist
journalist	music, English, foreign	occupational therapist
entertainer	languages)	speech pathologist
architect	psychologist	laboratory technologist
actor	counselor	public health nurse
editor	social worker	dental hygienist
reporter	librarian	physician
journalist	clergy	human resources
musician	religious educator	specialist
graphic designer	missionary	social scientist
art director	church worker	consultant

College majors

art	foreign languages	medicine
music	architecture	health occupations
graphic design	education	social work
journalism	religious studies	counseling
English	psychology	business

INTJ

INTJs are reserved, detached, analytical, logical, rational, original, independent, creative, ingenious, innovative, and resourceful. They prefer to work alone and work best alone. They can work with others if their ideas and competence are respected. They value knowledge and efficiency. They enjoy creative and intellectual challenges and understand complex theories. They create order and structure. They prefer to work with autonomy and control over their work. They dislike factual and routine kinds of work.

General occupations to consider

business and finance	education	law
technical occupations	health care and medicine	creative occupations
science	architecture	engineering

Specific job titles

management consultant	astronomer	dentist
human resources planner	computer programmer	biomedical engineer
economist	biomedical researcher	attorney
international banker	software developer	manager
financial planner	network integration	judge
investment banker	specialist	electrical engineer
scientist	teacher (university)	writer
scientific researcher	school principal	journalist
chemist	mathematician	artist
biologist	psychiatrist	inventor

computer systems analyst	psychologist	architect
electronic technician	neurologist	actor
design engineer	physician	musician
architect		

College majors

business	physics	journalism
finance	education	art
chemistry	mathematics	architecture
biology	medicine	drama
computers	psychology	music
engineering	law	vocational training
astronomy	English	

INTP

INTPs are logical, analytical, independent, original, creative, and insightful. They are often brilliant and ingenious. They work best alone and need quiet time to concentrate. They focus their attention on ideas and are frequently detached from other people. They love theory and abstract ideas and value knowledge and competency. INTPs are creative thinkers who are not too interested in practical application. They dislike detail and routine and need freedom to develop, analyze, and critique new ideas. These types maintain high standards in their work.

General occupations to consider

planning and	technical	academic
development	professional	creative occupations
health care		

Specific job titles

computer software	pharmacist	historian
designer	engineer	philosopher
computer programmer	electrician	college teacher
research and development	dentist	researcher
systems analyst	veterinarian	logician
financial planner	lawyer	photographer
investment banker	economist	creative writer
physicist	psychologist	artist
plastic surgeon	architect	actor
psychiatrist	psychiatrist	entertainer
chemist	mathematician	musician
biologist	archaeologist	inventor
pharmaceutical researcher		

College majors

computers	philosophy	mathematics
business	music	archaeology
physics	art	history
chemistry	drama	English
biology	engineering	drama
astronomy	psychology	music
medicine	architecture	vocational training

ESTP

ESTPs have great people skills and are action-oriented, fun, flexible, adaptable, and resourceful. They enjoy new experiences and dealing with people. They remember facts easily and have excellent powers of observation that they use to analyze other people. They are good problem solvers and can react quickly in an emergency. They like adventure and risk and are alert to new opportunities. They start new projects but do not necessarily follow through to completion. They prefer environments without too many rules and restrictions.

General occupations to consider

sales	entertainment	technical
service	sports	trade
active careers	health care	business
finance		

Specific job titles

marketing professional	insurance agent	dentist
firefighter	sportscaster	carpenter
police officer	news reporter	farmer
corrections officer	journalist	construction worker
paramedic	tour agent	electrician
detective	dancer	teacher (trade, industrial,
pilot	bartender	technical)
investigator	auctioneer	chef
real estate agent	professional athlete or	engineer
exercise physiologist	coach	surveyor
flight attendant	fitness instructor	radiologic technician
sports merchandise sales	recreation leader	entrepreneur
stockbroker	optometrist	land developer
financial planner	pharmacist	retail sales
investor	critical care nurse	car sales

College majors

business	vocational training	English
physical education	education	journalism
health occupations		

ESTJ

ESTJs are loyal, hardworking, dependable, thorough, practical, realistic, and energetic. They value security and tradition. Because they enjoy working with people and are orderly and organized, these types like to take charge and be the leader. This personality type is often found in administrative and management positions. ESTJs work systematically and efficiently to get the job done. These types are fair, logical, and consistent. They prefer a stable and predictable environment filled with action and a variety of people.

General occupations to consider

managerial	service	professional
sales	technical	military leaders
business	agriculture	

Specific job titles

retail store manager
fire department manager
small business manager
restaurant manager
financial or bank officer
school principal
sales manager
top-level manager in city/
    county/state
    government
management consultant
corporate executive

military officer or enlistee
office manager
purchasing agent
police officer
factory supervisor
corrections
insurance agent
detective
judge
accountant
nursing administrator
mechanical engineer

physician
chemical engineer
auditor
coach
public relations worker
cook
personnel or labor
    relations worker
teacher (trade, industrial,
    technical)
mortgage banker

College majors

business
business management
accounting
finance

small business
    management
engineering
agriculture

law
education
vocational training

ESFP

ESFPs are practical, realistic, independent, fun, social, spontaneous, and flexible. They have great people skills and enjoy working in environments that are friendly, relaxed, and varied. They know how to have a good time and make an environment fun for others. ESFPs have a strong sense of aesthetics and are sometimes artistic and creative. They often have a special bond with people or animals. They dislike structure and routine. These types can handle many activities or projects at once.

General occupations to consider

education
social service
food preparation

health care
entertainment
child care

business and sales
service

Specific job titles

child care worker
teacher (preschool,
    elementary school,
    foreign languages,
    mathematics)
athletic coach
counselor
library assistant
police officer
public health nurse
respiratory therapist
physical therapist
physician
emergency medical
    technician
dental hygienist
chef

medical assistant
critical care nurse
dentist
dental assistant
exercise physiologist
dog obedience trainer
veterinary assistant
travel or tour agent
recreation leader or
    amusement site worker
photographer
designer
film producer
musician
performer
actor

promoter
special events coordinator
editor or reporter
retail merchandiser
fund raiser
receptionist
real estate agent
insurance agent
sporting equipment sales
retail sales
retail management
waiter or waitress
cashier
cosmetologist
hairdresser
religious worker

College majors

education
psychology
foreign languages
mathematics
physical education
culinary arts

health occupations
art
design
photography
English
child development

journalism
drama
music
business
vocational training

ESFJ

ESFJs are friendly, organized, hardworking, productive, conscientious, loyal, dependable, and practical. These types value harmony, stability, and security. They enjoy interacting with people and receive satisfaction from giving to others. ESFJs enjoy working in a cooperative environment in which people get along well with each other. They create order, structure, and schedules and can be depended on to complete the task at hand. They prefer to organize and control their work.

General occupations to consider

health care
education
child care

social service
counseling

business
human resources

Specific job titles

medical or dental assistant
nurse
radiologic technician
dental hygienist
speech pathologist
occupational therapist
dentist
optometrist
dietician
pharmacist
physician
physical therapist
health education
   practitioner
medical secretary
teacher (grades 1–12,
   foreign languages,
   reading)

coach
administrator of
   elementary
   or secondary school
administrator of student
   personnel
child care provider
home economist
social worker
administrator of social
   services
police officer
counselor
community welfare
   worker
religious educator
clergy

sales representative
hairdresser
cosmetologist
restaurant worker
recreation or amusement
   site worker
receptionist
office manager
cashier
bank employee
bookkeeper
accountant
sales
insurance agent
credit counselor
merchandise planner

College majors

health occupations
biology
foreign languages
English

education
psychology
counseling
sociology

religious studies
business
vocational training
child development

ENFP

ENFPs are friendly, creative, energetic, enthusiastic, innovative, adventurous, and fun. They have great people skills and enjoy providing service to others. They are intuitive and perceptive about people. ENFPs are good at anything that interests them and can enter a variety of fields. These types dislike routine and detailed tasks and may have difficulty following through and completing tasks. They enjoy occupations in which they can be creative and interact with people. They like a friendly and relaxed environment in which they are free to follow their inspiration and participate in adventures.

General occupations to consider

creative occupations	counseling	social service
marketing	health care	entrepreneurial business
education	religious services	arts
environmental science		

Specific job titles

journalist	public relations	physical therapist
musician	counselor	consultant
actor	clergy	inventor
entertainer	psychologist	sales
fine artist	teacher (health, special	human resources
playwright	education, English, art,	manager
newscaster	drama, music)	conference planner
reporter	social worker	employment development
interior decorator	dental hygienist	specialist
cartoonist	nurse	restaurateur
graphic designer	dietician	merchandise planner
marketing	holistic health practitioner	environmental attorney
advertising	environmentalist	lawyer

College majors

journalism	business (advertising,	religious studies
English	marketing, public	health occupations
drama	relations)	law
art	counseling	vocational training
graphic design	psychology	

ENFJ

ENFJs are friendly, sociable, empathetic, loyal, creative, imaginative, and responsible. They have great people skills and are interested in working with people and providing service to them. They are good at building harmony and cooperation and respect other people's opinions. These types can find creative solutions to problems. They are natural leaders who can make good decisions. They prefer an environment that is organized and structured and enjoy working as part of a team with other creative and caring people.

General occupations to consider

religious occupations	counseling	health care
creative occupations	education	business
communications	human services	administration

Specific job titles

director of religious education
minister
clergy
public relations
marketing
writer
librarian
journalist
fine artist
designer
actor
musician or composer
fundraiser
recreational director
TV producer

newscaster
politician
editor
crisis counselor
school counselor
vocational or career counselor
psychologist
alcohol and drug counselor
teacher (health, art, drama, English, foreign languages)
child care worker
college humanities professor

social worker
home economist
nutritionist
speech pathologist
occupational therapist
physical therapist
optometrist
dental hygienist
family practice physician
psychiatrist
nursing educator
pharmacist
human resources trainer
travel agent
small business executive
sales manager

College majors

religious studies
business (public relations, marketing)
art
graphic design
drama

music
journalism
English
foreign languages
humanities
psychology

counseling
sociology
health occupations
business
vocational training

ENTP

ENTPs are creative, ingenious, flexible, diverse, energetic, fun, motivating, logical, and outspoken. They have excellent people skills and are natural leaders, although they dislike controlling other people. They value knowledge and competence. They are lively and energetic and make good debaters and motivational speakers. They are logical and rational thinkers who can grasp complex ideas and theories. They dislike environments that are structured and rigid. These types prefer environments that allow them to engage in creative problem solving and the creation of new ideas.

General occupations to consider

creative occupations
politics
engineering

law
business
science

health care
architecture
education

Specific job titles

photographer
marketing professional
journalist
actor
writer
musician or composer
editor
reporter
advertising director
radio/TV talk show host
producer

politician
political manager
political analyst
social scientist
psychiatrist
psychologist
engineer
construction laborer
research worker
electrician
lawyer

computer professional
corrections officer
sales manager
speech pathologist
health education practitioner
respiratory therapist
dental assistant
medical assistant
critical care nurse
counselor

art director	judge	human resources planner
new business developer	corporate executive	educator
architect		

College majors

art	music	political science
photography	business (advertising,	psychology
journalism	marketing,	health occupations
drama	management,	computers
English	human resources)	vocational training
engineering	architecture	education
science		

ENTJ

ENTJs are independent, original, visionary, logical, organized, ambitious, competitive, hardworking, and direct. They are natural leaders and organizers who identify problems and create solutions for organizations. ENTJs are often in management positions. They are good planners and accomplish goals in a timely manner. These types are logical thinkers who enjoy a structured work environment where they have opportunity for advancement. They enjoy a challenging, competitive, and exciting environment in which accomplishments are recognized.

General occupations to consider

| business | management | science |
| finance | health care | law |

Specific job titles

executive	manager in city/county/	accountant
manager	state government	auditor
supervisor	management trainer	financial manager
personnel manager	school principal	real estate agent
sales manager	bank officer	lawyer, judge
marketing manager	computer systems analyst	consultant
human resources planner	computer professional	engineer
corporate executive	credit investigator	corrections, probation
college administrator	mortgage broker	officer
health administrator	stockbroker	psychologist
small business owner	investment banker	physician
retail store manager	economist	

College majors

business management	computers	engineering
finance	law	psychology
economics	medicine	vocational training

Summing Up Values

Name _____ Date _____

Look at the "Values Checklist" you completed in this chapter. Choose the 10 values most important to you and list them here.

_____   _____

_____   _____

_____   _____

_____   _____

_____   _____

Next, pick out the value that is most important and label it 1. Label your second most important value 2, and so on, until you have picked out your top five values.

1. My most important value is _____.
   Why?

2. My second most important value is _____.
   Why?

3. My third most important value is _____.
   Why?

How Can I Set Attainable and Realistic Goals for My Future?

Learning Objectives

Read to answer these key questions:

- How can I make good decisions about my future?

- What are my goals for the future?

Thinking as a Developmental Process

Cognitive psychologists study the development and organization of knowledge and the role it plays in various mental activities (e.g., reading, writing, decision making, and problem solving). What is knowledge? Where it is stored? How do you construct mental representations of your world? The personal answers to these and other questions are often found for the first time in college when students focus their attention on what they know and how they know it.

Models of Knowledge

Different forms of knowledge interact when you reason and construct mental representation of the situation before you, and different situations require different levels of thinking. How you learn and study chemistry is likely very different from the way you approach political science or calculus. Joanne Kurfiss (1988) wrote about the following three kinds of knowledge:

- **Declarative knowledge** is knowing facts and concepts. Kurfiss recognizes the considerable amount of declarative knowledge that students acquire through their college courses. To move students to a higher level of thinking, instructors generally ask students to write analytical essays, instead of mere summaries, to explain the knowledge they have acquired in the course.
- **Procedural knowledge**, or strategic knowledge, is knowing how to use declarative knowledge to do something (e.g., interpret textbooks, study, navigate the Internet, and find a major).
- **Metacognition** is knowing what knowledge to use to control one's situation (e.g., how to make plans, ask questions, analyze the effectiveness of learning strategies, initiate change). If students' metacognitive skills are not well developed, students may not be able to use the full potential of their knowledge when studying in college.

William Perry

You read about the developmental theorist William Perry earlier in this textbook. In his research on college-age students, Perry distinguished a series of stages that students pass through as they move from simple to complex levels of thinking. Basically, they move from dualism, the simplest stage, where knowledge is viewed as a factual quality dispensed by authorities (professors), to multiplicity, in which the student recognizes the complexity of knowledge (e.g., he or she understands that there is more than one perspective of the bombing of Hiroshima or the role of the United States in the Vietnam War) and believes knowledge to be subjective, to relativism, where the student reaches an understanding that some views make greater sense than other views. Relativism is reflected in situations where a student has made a commitment to the particular view they have constructed of the world, also known as Weltanschauung. Constructing a personal critical epistemology is an essential developmental task for undergraduates, according to Perry (Chaffee, 1998).

Bloom's Taxonomy of Thinking and Learning

Benjamin Bloom (1956) and his associates at the University of Chicago developed a classification system, or taxonomy, to explain how we think and learn (see Figure 6.1). The taxonomy consists of six levels of thinking arranged in a hierarchy, beginning with simple cognitive tasks (knowledge) and moving up to more complex thinking (evaluation).

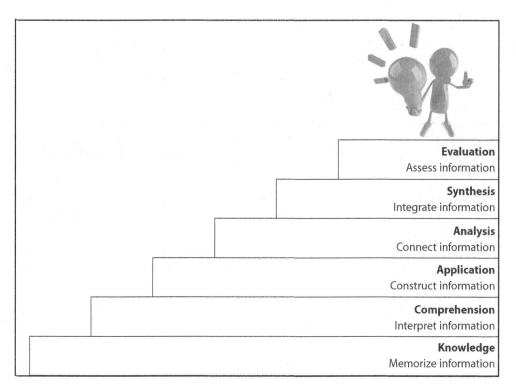

Figure 6.1
Bloom's Taxonomy of
Thinking.

Thinking at each level is dependent on thinking skills at lower levels. One of the reasons that college students often experience difficulty learning and studying during their first semester is that the learning and study strategies from high school are not necessarily effective in the new setting. In high school, you are generally asked to memorize and interpret information. In college, you are asked to do all that and more. To be successful in a college setting, you need to learn how to apply, analyze, synthesize, and evaluate information. Let's look at Bloom's six levels of learning and thinking, beginning with the lowest level of thinking.

KNOWLEDGE LEVEL. If you are cramming for a test, chances are good that you are thinking at the knowledge level, the lowest level of thinking. You are basically attempting to memorize a lot of information in a short amount of time. If you are asked on the test to identify, name, select, define, or list particular bits of information, you might do okay, but you will most likely forget most of the information soon after taking the test.

COMPREHENSION LEVEL. When you are classifying, describing, discussing, explaining, and recognizing information, you are in the process of interpreting information. At the bottom of your lecture notes for the day, see if you can summarize your notes using your own words. By doing so, you can develop a deeper understanding of the material just covered in class.

APPLICATION LEVEL. At this third level of thinking, you are constructing knowledge by taking previously learned information and applying it in a new and different way to solve problems. Whenever you use a formula or a theory to solve a problem, you are thinking at the application level. Some words used to describe how you process information at this level are *illustrate*, *demonstrate*, and *apply*. To increase thinking at the application level, develop the habit of thinking of examples to illustrate concepts presented in class or during reading. Be sure to include the examples in your notations in your books and notes.

ANALYSIS LEVEL. When you analyze information, you break the information down into parts and then look at the relationships among the parts. In your literature class, if you read two plays from different time periods and then compare and contrast them in terms of style and form, you are analyzing. When you analyze, you connect pieces of information. You discriminate, correlate, classify, and infer.

SYNTHESIS LEVEL. When you are synthesizing information, you are bringing together all the bits of information that you have analyzed to create a new pattern or whole. When you synthesize, you hypothesize, predict, generate, and integrate. Innovative ideas often emerge at the synthesis level of thinking.

EVALUATION LEVEL. This is the highest level of thinking according to Bloom's taxonomy. When you evaluate, you judge the validity of the information. You may be evaluating opinions ("Is that person really an expert?") or biases.

Answer the following questions to test your understanding of Bloom's taxonomy. According to Bloom's taxonomy of thinking, which level of thinking would you be engaging in if you were asked to

- Read an article about an upcoming candidate in a local election and then summarize the candidate's characteristics?
- View a video about hate and prejudice and then write an essay about how you can confront hate and prejudice on a personal level?
- Read through the chapter in this book on learning styles and then determine the most effective way for you to study?
- Identify and define the parts of the forebrain?
- Judge a new campus parking policy created by your college's parking services?

Models of Critical Thinking/Problem Solving

Critical Thinking

One of the primary objectives of a college education is to develop the skills necessary to become an autonomous, independent learner. Critical thinking prepares you to be an independent thinker. Many models of critical thinking have been developed which can be used to develop strong critical thinking skills. One such model, developed by the authors of this textbook, is called CRITICAL (Glauser & Ginter, 1995). This model identifies important steps and key ideas in critical thinking: Construction, Refocus, Identity, Think through, Insight, Conclusions, Accuracy, and Lens.

CONSTRUCTION. Each of us constructs a unique view of the world. Our construction, or perception, of the world is based on our thoughts and beliefs. Our cultural background influences our perceptions, and they form the basis of our assumptions. For example, you might assume that a college education can help you to get a better job. How do you know this? Maybe you know this because a parent or teacher told you so. If this is the only bit of information on which you are basing your assumption about the value of a college education, you have not engaged in critical thinking. If you had engaged in critical thinking, you would have analyzed and synthesized information that you gathered about the benefits of a college education. If you have based your decision to attend this college on good critical thinking, then you will know why you are here and will more likely be motivated to graduate.

Perceptions of information, behaviors, and situations are often based on unexamined assumptions that are inaccurate and sketchy. The first step in this model is to investigate personal underlying biases that are inherent in your assumptions about any issue before you. For example, let us say that you are with some friends and the topic of surrogate motherhood comes up. Maybe you have already formed an opinion about the issue. This opinion could be based on strong critical thinking, but if not, then your opinion is merely a strong personal feeling. If you choose to look at surrogate motherhood from a critical-thinking perspective, you would begin by examining your own thoughts and beliefs about motherhood and surrogacy. No matter what issue is before you (e.g., racism, economic downturn, environmental pollution, abortion, euthanasia, genetic engineering), the process is the same: begin by examining your own assumptions. As you do this, look for biases and other patterns of thinking that have become cemented over time and are influencing the way you view the issue.

REFOCUS. Once you have acknowledged some of your own biases, refocus your attention so you can hear alternative viewpoints. Refocus by reading additional information, talking to people with opposing viewpoints, or maybe watching a movie. You are trying to see other people's perspectives. Read carefully, and listen carefully with the intent to learn. Can you think of any books that you have read or movies that have influenced the way you see a particular issue?

To illustrate the effect of refocusing, list three sources of additional information (e.g., a book, a movie, another person, a newspaper article, or an experience) that changed your mind about something important to you. Explain how each changed you.

1. _____
_____
_____

2. _____
_____
_____

3. _____
_____
_____

IDENTIFY. Identifying core issues and information is the third step of critical thinking. After you have gathered all your additional information representing different viewpoints, think over the information carefully. Are there any themes that emerge? What does the terminology related to the issue tell you? Look at all the facts and details. We all try to make sense out of what we hear and see by arranging information into a pattern, a story that seems reasonable. There is a tendency to arrange the information to fit our perceptions and beliefs. When we engage in critical thinking, we are trying to make sense of all the pieces, not just the ones that happen to fit our own preconceived pattern.

THINK THROUGH. The fourth step of critical thinking requires that you think through all the information gathered. The task is to distinguish between what is fact and what is fiction and what is relevant and not relevant. Examine premises and decide if they are logically valid. Look for misinformation. Maybe you have gathered inaccurate facts and figures. Check the sources for reliability. Asking questions is a large part of good critical thinking.

This step of the model is where you analyze and synthesize information. You are continually focusing your attention in and out, in the same way that you might focus a camera. This step of the critical-thinking process can be very creative. You are using both parts of the brain. The right brain is being speculative, suspending judgment, and challenging definitions. The left brain is analyzing the information received in a more traditional style, thinking logically and sequentially. While thinking critically, have you detected any overgeneralizations (e.g., women are more emotional and less rational than men) or oversimplifications (e.g., the high dropout rate at the local high school is due to an increase in single-parent families)?

INSIGHT. Once key issues have been identified and analyzed, it is time to develop some insight into some of the various perspectives on the issue. Sometimes some of the best insights come when you can sit back and detach yourself from all the information you have just processed. Often new meanings will emerge that provide a new awareness. You might find that you have developed some empathy for others that may not have been there before. When you hear the term "broken home," what images do you conjure up? How do you think a child who resides with a single parent or alternates between divorced parents' homes feels when hearing that term applied to his or her situation? A lot of assumptions are embedded in such concepts.

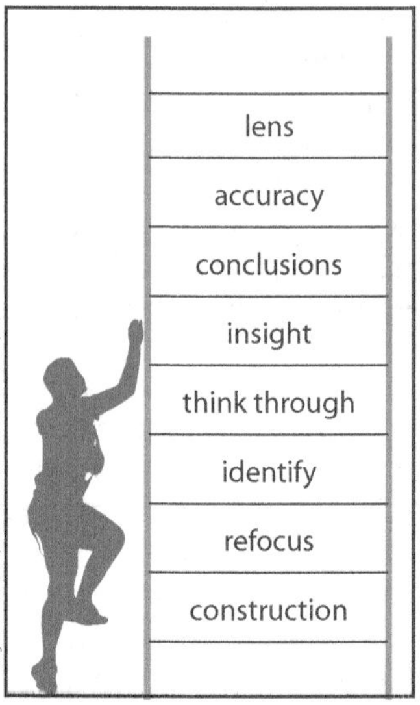

CONCLUSIONS. If you do not have sufficient evidence to support a decision, suspend judgment until you do. An important tenet of critical thinking is not to jump to conclusions. If you do, you may find that you have a fallacy in your reasoning. A fallacy is an instance of incorrect reasoning. Maybe you did not have sufficient evidence to support your decision to major in biology, or maybe your conclusions about the issue of euthanasia do not follow logically from your premise. Also, look at the conclusions you have drawn, and ask yourself if they have any implications that you might need to rethink. Do you need to consider alternative interpretations of the evidence?

Figure 6.2
CRITICAL Model.

ACCURACY. You are not through thinking! In addition to looking for fallacies in your reasoning, you also need to consider some other things:

- Know the difference between reasoning and rationalizing. Which thinking processes are your conclusions based on?
- Know the difference between what is true and what seems true based on the emotional attachment you have to your ideas and beliefs.
- Know the difference between opinion and fact. Facts can be proven; opinions cannot.

LENS. In this last step of critical thinking, you have reached the understanding that most issues can be viewed from multiple perspectives. These perspectives form a lens that offers a more encompassing view of the world around you. Remember that there are usually many solutions to a single issue.

Problem Solving

Problem solving involves critical thinking. Are problem solving and critical thinking the same? Not really. Problem solving is about having the ability and skills to apply knowledge to pragmatic problems encountered in all areas of your life. If you were trying to solve a financial problem or decide whether or not to change roommates, you probably would not need a model of thinking as extensive as the one previously described. The following steps offer an organized approach to solving less complex problems:

1. Identify the problem. Be specific and write it down.
2. Analyze the problem.
3. Identify alternative ways to solve the problem.
4. Examine alternatives.
5. Implement a solution.
6. Evaluate.

IDENTIFY THE PROBLEM. What exactly is the problem you wish to solve? Is it that your roommate is driving you crazy, or is it that you want to move into an apartment with your friend next semester? Be specific.

ANALYZE THE PROBLEM. Remember, analysis means looking at all the parts. It is the process by which we select and interpret information. Be careful not to be too selective or simplistic in your thinking. Look at all the facts and details. For example, suppose you want to move into an apartment with your friends. Do you need permission from anyone to do so? Can you afford to do this? Can you get a release from your residence hall? Your answer to all the questions might be yes, with the exception of being able to afford it. You want to move, so now the problem is a financial one. You need to come up with the financial resources to follow through on your decision.

IDENTIFY ALTERNATIVE WAYS TO SOLVE THE PROBLEM. Use convergent and divergent thinking. You are engaging in convergent thinking when you are narrowing choices to come up with the correct solution (e.g., picking the best idea out of three). You are engaging in **divergent thinking** when you are thinking in terms of multiple solutions. Mihaly Csikszentmihalyi (1996) says, "Divergent thinking leads to no agreed-upon solution. It involves fluency, or the ability to generate a great quantity of ideas; flexibility, or the ability to switch from one perspective to another; and originality in picking unusual associations of ideas" (p. 60). He concludes that a person whose thinking has these qualities is likely to come up with more innovative ideas.

Brainstorming is a great way to generate alternative ways to solve problems. This creative problem-solving technique requires that you use both divergent and convergent thinking. Here are some steps to use if you decide to brainstorm.

1. Describe the problem.
2. Decide on the amount of time you want to spend brainstorming (e.g., ten minutes).
3. Relax (remember, some of the best insights come in a relaxed state).
4. Write down everything that comes to your mind (divergent thinking).
5. Select your best ideas (convergent thinking).
6. Try one out! (If it does not work, try one of the other ideas you selected.)

Students have successfully used the process of brainstorming to decide on a major, select internships, develop topics for papers, and come up with ideas for part-time jobs. Being creative means coming up with atypical solutions to complex problems.

EXAMINE ALTERNATIVES. How do you decide among the alternatives? Make judgments about the alternatives based on previous knowledge and the additional information you now have.

IMPLEMENT A SOLUTION. Choose one solution to your problem and eliminate the others for now (if this one fails, you may want to try another solution later).

EVALUATE. If the plan is not as effective as you had hoped, modify your plan or start the process over again. Also, look at the criteria you used to judge your alternative solutions.

Think of a problem that you are currently dealing with and complete Exercise 2 ("Creating Breakthroughs") at the end of the chapter. This is an opportunity to try to solve a problem using this six-step problem-solving model.

Arguments

Critical thinking involves the construction and evaluation of arguments. An **argument** is a form of thinking in which reasons (statements and facts) are given in support of a conclusion. The reasons of the argument are known as the **premises**. A good argument is one in which the premises are logical and support the conclusion. The validity of the argument is based on the relationship between the premises and the conclusion. If the premises are not credible or do not support the conclusion, or the conclusion does not follow from the premises, the argument is considered to be **invalid** or **fallacious**. **Unsound arguments** (based on fallacies) are often persuasive because they can appeal to our emotions and confirm what we want to believe to be true. Just look at commercials on television. Alcohol advertisements show that you can be rebellious, independent, and have lots of friends, fun, and excitement by drinking large quantities of alcohol—all without any negative consequences. Intelligence is reflected in the capacity to acquire and apply knowledge. Even sophisticated, intelligent people are influenced by fallacious advertising.

Invalid Arguments

It is human irrationality, not a lack of knowledge, that threatens human potential.

—Raymond Nickerson, in J. K. Kurfiss, *Critical Thinking*

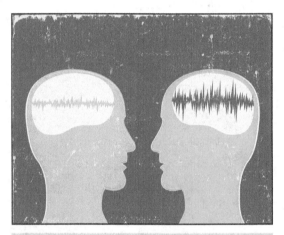

Critical Thinking Makes a Difference.

In the book *How to Think about Weird Things*, Theodore Schick and Lewis Vaughn (1999) suggest that you can avoid holding irrational beliefs by understanding the ways in which an argument can fail. First, an argument is fallacious if it contains **unacceptable premises**, premises that are as incredible as the claim they are supposed to support. Second, if it contains **irrelevant premises**, or premises that are not logically related to the conclusion, it is also fallacious. Third, it is fallacious if it contains **insufficient premises**, meaning that the premises do not eliminate reasonable grounds for doubt. Schick and Vaughn recommend that whenever someone presents an argument, you check to see if the premises are acceptable, relevant, and sufficient. If not, then the argument presented is not logically compelling or valid.

Schick and Vaughn abstracted from the work of Ludwig F. Schlecht the following examples of fallacies based on illogical premises:

Unacceptable Premises

- **False dilemma** (also known as the either/or fallacy) presumes that there are only two alternatives from which to choose when in actuality there are more than two. For example: You are either with America or against us. You are not with America, therefore you are against us.
- **Begging the question** is also referred to as arguing in a circle. A conclusion is used as one of the premises. For example: "You should major in business, because my advisor says that if you do, you will be guaranteed a job." "How do you know this?" "My advisor told me that all business majors find jobs."

Irrelevant Premises

- **Equivocation** occurs when the conclusion does not follow from the premises due to using the same word to mean two different things. For example: Senator Dobbs has always been *patriotic* and shown a deep affection and respect for his country. Now, though, he is criticizing the government's foreign policy. This lack of *patriotism* makes him unworthy of reelection.

- **Appeal to the person** (*ad hominem*, or "to the man") occurs when a person offers a rebuttal to an argument by criticizing or denigrating its presenter rather than constructing a rebuttal based on the argument presented. As Schick and Vaughn note, "Crazy people can come up with perfectly sound arguments, and sane people can talk nonsense" (1999, p. 287).
- **Appeal to authority** is when we support our views by citing experts. If the person is truly an expert in the field for which they are being cited, then the testimony is probably valid. How often do you see celebrities endorsing products? Is an argument valid just because someone cites an article from the *New York Times* or the *Wall Street Journal* for support?
- **Appeal to the masses** is a type of fallacy that occurs when support for the premise is offered in the form, "It must be right because everybody else does it." For example: It's okay to cheat. Every college student cheats sometime during their undergraduate years.
- **Appeal to tradition** is used as an unsound premise when we argue that something is true based on an established tradition. For example: It's okay to drink large quantities of alcohol and go wild during spring break. It's what students have always done.
- **Appeal to ignorance** relies on claims that if no proof is offered that something is true, then it must be false, or conversely, that if no proof is offered that something is false, then it must be true. Many arguments associated with religions of the world are based on irrelevant premises that appeal to ignorance.
- **Appeal to fear** is based on a threat, or "swinging the big stick." For example: If you don't start studying now, you will never make it through college. Schick and Vaughn remind us, "Threats extort; they do not help us arrive at the truth" (1999, p. 289).

Insufficient Premises

- **Hasty generalizations** are often seen when people stereotype others. Have you noticed that most stereotypes are negative? When we describe an individual as pushy, cheap, aggressive, privileged, snobbish, or clannish and then generalize that attribute to the group we believe that person belongs to, we are committing a hasty generalization.
- **Faulty analogy** is the type of fallacy committed when there is a claim that things that have similar qualities in some respects will have similarities in other respects. For example: Dr. Smith and Dr. Wilson may both teach at the same college, but their individual philosophies about teaching and learning may be very different.
- **False cause** fallacies occur when a causal relationship is assumed despite a lack of evidence to support the relationship. Do you have a special shirt or hat that you wear on game days to influence the odds that the team you are cheering for wins?

Crop Circles

Crop circles are swirled patterns of bent-over plants, such as wheat, corn, or soybeans, that mysteriously appear in large fields. First noticed in southern England, crop circles have started to appear all over the world. They range from simple, circular shapes to elaborate pictograms. Originally, some thought that the circles were produced by extraterrestrials or some other paranormal phenomenon. Others thought that they were produced by "plasma vortex phenomena" that consisted of a spinning mass of air containing electrically charged matter. Still others thought that they were produced by clever human beings.

In 1991, two pub mates in their sixties—Doug Bower and Dave Chorley—claimed to have produced many of the English crop circles by attaching a rope to both ends of a long narrow plank, holding it between themselves and the plants, and stepping on the plank to bend over the plants. To substantiate their claim, they produced a circle for a tabloid newspaper, which was later claimed to be of extraterrestrial origin by one of the believers in the extraterrestrial hypothesis. Since then, other crop circles thought impossible to hoax have turned out to be manmade. Apparently there is no reliable way to distinguish crop circles of terrestrial origin from those of extraterrestrial origin. Nevertheless, people continue to believe that crop circles are messages from outer space.

Making Good Decisions

© 2014, Anastasia vish. Used under license with Shutterstock, Inc.

Knowing how to make a good decision about your career and important life events is very important to your future, as this short poem by J. Wooden sums up:

There is a choice you have to make, In everything you do

And you must always keep in mind, The choice you make, makes you.[1]

Sometimes people end up in a career because they simply seized an opportunity for employment. A good job becomes available and they happen to be in the right place at the right time. Sometimes people end up in a career because it is familiar to them, because it is a job held by a member of the family or a friend in the community. Sometimes people end up in a career because of economic necessity. The job pays well and they need the money. These careers are the result of chance circumstances. Sometimes they turn out well, and sometimes they turn out miserably.

Whether you are male or female, married or single, you will spend a great deal of your life working. By doing some careful thinking and planning about your career, you can improve your chances of success and happiness. Use the following steps to do some careful decision making about your career. Although you are the person who needs to make the decision about a career, you can get help from your college career center or your college counselor or advisor.

Steps in Making a Career Decision

1. **Begin with self-assessment.**
   - What is your personality type?
   - What are your interests?
   - What are your talents, gifts, and strengths?
   - What is your learning style?
   - What are your values?
   - What lifestyle do you prefer?

2. **Explore your options.**
   - What careers match your personal characteristics?

3. **Research your career options.**
   - Read the job description.
   - Investigate the career outlook.
   - What is the salary?
   - What training and education is required?
   - Speak with an advisor, counselor, or person involved in the career that interests you.
   - Choose a career or general career area that matches your personal characteristics.

4. **Plan your education to match your career goal.**
   - Try out courses in your area of interest.
   - Start your general education if you need more time to decide on a major.
   - Try an internship or part-time job in your area of interest.

5. **Make a commitment to take action and follow through with your plan.**

6. **Evaluate.**
   - Do you like the courses you are taking?
   - Are you doing well in the courses?
   - Continue research if necessary.

7. **Refine your plan.**
   - Make your plan more specific to aim for a particular career.
   - Select the college major that is best for you.

8. **Change your plan if it is not working.**
   - Go back to the self-assessment step.

The Decision-Making Process

- **Dependent decisions.** Different kinds of decisions are appropriate in different situations. When you make a dependent decision, you depend on someone else to make the decision for you. The dependent decision was probably the first kind of decision that you ever made. When your parents told you what to do as a child, you were making a dependent decision. As an adult, you make a dependent decision when your doctor tells you what medication to take for an illness or when your stockbroker tells you what stock you should purchase. Dependent decisions are easy to make and require little thought. Making a dependent decision saves time and energy.

  The dependent decision, however, has some disadvantages. You may not like the outcome of the decision. The medication that your doctor prescribes may have unpleasant side effects. The stock that you purchased may go down in value. When students ask a counselor to recommend a major or a career, they are making a dependent decision. When the decision does not work, they blame the counselor. Even if the dependent decision does have good results, you may become dependent on others to continue making decisions for you. Dependent decisions do work in certain situations, but they do not give you as much control over your own life.

- **Intuitive decisions.** Intuitive decisions are based on intuition or a gut feeling about what is the best course of action. Intuitive decisions can be made quickly and are useful in dealing with emergencies. If I see a car heading on a collision path toward me, I have to swerve quickly to the right or left. I do not have time to ask someone else what to do or think much about the alternatives. Another example of an intuitive decision is in gambling. If I am trying to decide whether to bet a dollar on red or black, I rely on my gut feeling to make a choice. Intuitive decisions may work out or they may not. You could make a mistake and swerve the wrong way as the car approaches or you could lose your money in gambling.

- **Planful decisions.** For important decisions, it is advantageous to use what is called a planful decision. The planful decision is made after carefully weighing the consequences and the pros and cons of the different alternatives. The planful decision-making strategy is particularly useful for such decisions as:
  - What will be my major?
  - What career should I choose?
  - Whom should I marry?

> "Find a job you like and add five days to every week".
>
> H. Jackson Browne

The steps in a planful decision-making process:

1. **State the problem.** When we become aware of a problem, the first step is to state the problem in the simplest way possible. Just stating the problem will help you to clarify the issues.

2. **Consider your values.** What is important to you? What are your hopes and dreams? By keeping your values in mind, you are more likely to make a decision that will make you happy.

3. **What are your talents?** What special skills do you have? How can you make a decision that utilizes these skills?

4. **Gather information.** What information can you find that would be helpful in solving the problem? Look for ideas. Ask other people. Do some research. Gathering information can give you insight into alternatives or possible solutions to the problem.

5. **Generate alternatives.** Based on the information you have gathered, identify some possible solutions to the problem.

6. **Evaluate the pros and cons of each alternative.** List the alternatives and think about the pros and cons of each one. In thinking about the pros and cons, consider your values and talents as well as your future goals.

7. **Select the best alternative.** Choose the alternative that is the best match for your values and helps you to achieve your goals.

8. **Take action.** You put your decision into practice when you take some action on it. Get started!

What Are My Lifetime Goals?

You have now completed the assessment part of the course and have a greater awareness of your personal strengths, vocational interests, values, and multiple intelligences. Use this knowledge to begin thinking about some goals for the future.

Setting goals helps you to establish what is important and provides direction for your life. Goals help you to focus your energy on what you want to accomplish. Goals are a promise to yourself to improve your life. Setting goals can help you turn your dreams into reality. Steven Scott in his book, *A Millionaire's Notebook,* lays out five steps in this process:

1. Dream or visualize.

2. Convert the dream into goals.

3. Convert your goals into tasks.

4. Convert your task into steps.

5. Take your first step and then the next.[2]

As you begin to think about your personal goals in life, make your goals specific and concrete. Rather than saying, "I want to be rich," make your goal something that you can break into specific steps. You might want to start learning about money management or begin a savings plan. Rather than setting a goal for happiness, think about what brings you happiness. If you want to live a long and healthy life, think about the health habits that will help you to accomplish your goal. You will need to break your goals down into specific tasks to be able to accomplish them.

Here are some criteria for successful goal setting:

1. **Is it achievable?** Do I have the skills, abilities, and resources to accomplish this goal? If not, am I willing to spend the time to develop the skills, abilities, and resources needed to achieve this goal?

2. **Is it realistic?** Do I believe I can achieve it? Am I positive and optimistic about this goal?

3. **Is it specific and measurable?** Can it be counted or observed? The most common goal mentioned by students is happiness in life. What is happiness, and how will you know when you have achieved it? Is happiness a career you enjoy, owning your own home, or a travel destination?

4. **Do you want to do it?** Is this a goal you are choosing because it gives you personal satisfaction rather than meeting a requirement or an expectation of someone else?

5. **Are you motivated to achieve it?** What are your rewards for achieving it?

6. **Does the goal match your values?** Is it important to you?

7. **What steps do you need to take to begin?** Am I willing to take action to start working on it?

8. **When will you finish this goal?** Set a date to accomplish your goal.

> "A goal is a dream with a deadline."
>
> Napoleon Hill

REFLECTION

Write a paragraph about your lifetime goals. Use any of these questions to guide your thinking:

What is your career goal? If you do not know what your career goal is, describe your preferred work environment. Would your ideal career require a college degree?

What are your family goals? Are you interested in marriage and family? What would be your important family values?

What are your social goals (friends, community, and recreation)?

When you are older and look back on your life, what are the three most important life goals that you would want to make sure to accomplish?

What Have I Learned from UNI 150 and What Are My Next Steps?

Learning Objectives

Read to answer these key questions:

- How does positive thinking affect my future success?

- What are some beliefs of successful people?

- What are some secrets to achieving happiness?

College students begin their college education with the dream of having a better future and achieving happiness in life. This chapter includes some tools for thinking positively about your future, analyzing what happiness means, and taking the steps to achieve happiness in your life.

Thinking Positively about Your Career

You have assessed your personal strengths, interests, and values and are on your way to choosing a major and career that will achieve your goals and make you happy in life. It is interesting to note that thoughts about work often determine whether it is just a job, a career, or a calling that makes life interesting and fulfilling. For example, consider the parable of the bricklayers:

> Three bricklayers are asked: "What are you doing?"
> The first says, "I am laying bricks."
> The second says, "I am building a church."
> The third says, "I am building the house of God."[1]

The first bricklayer has a job, the second one has a career, and the third one approaches his job with a sense of purpose and optimism; he has a calling. Depending on your thoughts, any career can be a job, a career, or a calling. You can find your calling by thinking about your purpose and how your job makes the world a better place. Although purposes are unique, you can analyze your beliefs about any job in this way and look for greater satisfaction in what you are doing. If your current work is not a calling, find ways to change or improve it to match your personal strengths and purpose. People who have found their calling are consistently happier than those who have a job or even a career.

© kentoh/Shutterstock.com

Optimism, Hope, and Future-Mindedness

You can increase your chances of success by using three powerful tools: optimism, hope, and future-mindedness. These character traits lead to achievement in athletics, academics, careers, and even politics. They also have positive mental and physical effects. They reduce anxiety and depression as well as contributing to physical well-being. In addition, they aid in problem solving and searching out resources to solve problems. A simple definition of optimism is expecting good events to happen in the future and working to make them happen. Optimism leads to continued efforts to accomplish goals, whereas pessimism leads to giving up on accomplishing goals. A person who sets no goals for the future cannot be optimistic or hopeful.

Being hopeful is another way of thinking positively about the future. Hope is the expectation that tomorrow will be better than today.[2] When you face challenges, you learn from mistakes, expect a positive outcome, and work to overcome the challenge. It is the opposite of accepting failure, expecting the worst, and giving up. In this way hope is related to the growth mindset and perseverance, or grit. One research study showed for entering college freshmen, level of hope was a better predictor of college grades than standardized tests or high school grade point average.[3] Students who have a high level of hope set higher goals and work to attain them. If they are not successful, they think about what went wrong and learn from it, or change goals and move in a new direction with a renewed sense of hope for a positive future.

Future-mindedness is thinking about the future, expecting that desired events and outcomes will occur, and then acting in a way that makes the positive outcomes come true. It involves setting goals for the future and taking action to accomplish these goals as well as being confident in accomplishing these goals. Individuals with future-mindedness are conscientious and hardworking and can delay gratification. They make to-do lists and use schedules and day planners. Individuals who are future-minded would agree with these statements:[4]

- Despite challenges, I always remain hopeful about the future.
- I always look on the bright side.
- I believe that good will always triumph over evil.
- I expect the best.
- I have a clear picture in mind about what I want to happen in the future.
- I have a plan for what I want to be doing five years from now.
- If I get a bad grade or evaluation, I focus on the next opportunity and plan to do better.

Believe in Yourself

Anthony Robbins defines belief as "any guiding principle, dictum, faith, or passion that can provide meaning and direction in life . . . Beliefs are the compass and maps that guide us toward our goals and give us the surety to know we'll get there."[5] The beliefs that we have about ourselves determine how much of our potential we will use and how successful we will be in the future. If we have positive beliefs about ourselves, we will feel confident and accomplish our goals in life. Negative beliefs get in the way of our success. Robbins reminds us that we can change our beliefs and choose new ones if necessary.

> *"The birth of excellence begins with our awareness that our beliefs are a choice. We usually do not think of it that way, but belief can be a conscious choice. You can choose beliefs that limit you, or you can choose beliefs that support you. The trick is to choose the beliefs that are conducive to success and the results you want and to discard the ones that hold you back."[6]*

> "Attitude is the librarian of our past, the speaker of our present and the prophet of our future."
> John Maxwell

> "¡Sí, se puede!" (Yes, you can!)
> César Chavez

The Self-Fulfilling Prophecy

The first step in thinking positively is to examine your beliefs about yourself, your life, and the world around you. Personal beliefs are influenced by our environment, significant events that have happened in life, what we have learned in the past, and our picture of the future. Beliefs cause us to have certain expectations about the world and ourselves. These expectations are such a powerful influence on behavior that psychologists use the term "self-fulfilling prophecy" to describe what happens when our expectations come true.

For example, if I believe that I am not good in math (my expectation), I may not try to do the assignment or may avoid taking a math class (my behavior). As a result, I am not good in math. My expectations have been fulfilled. Expectations can also have a positive effect. If I believe that I am a good student, I will take steps to enroll in college and complete my assignments. I will then become a good student. The prophecy will again come true.

> "If I believe I cannot do something, it makes me incapable of doing it. But when I believe I can, then I acquire the ability to do it, even if I did not have the ability in the beginning."
> Mahatma Gandhi

To think positively, it is necessary to recognize your negative beliefs and turn them into positive beliefs. Some negative beliefs commonly heard from college students include the following:

I don't have the money for college.
English was never my best subject.
I was never any good at math.

When you hear yourself saying these negative thoughts, remember that these thoughts can become self-fulfilling prophecies. First of all, notice the thought. Then see if you can change the statement into a positive statement such as:

I can find the money for college.
English has been a challenge for me in the past, but I will do better this time.
I can learn to be good at math.

If you believe that you can find money for college, you can go to the financial aid office and the scholarship office to begin your search for money to attend school. You can look for a better job or improve your money management. If you believe that you will do better in English, you will keep up with your assignments and go to the tutoring center or ask the professor for help. If you believe that you can learn to be good at math, you will attend every math class and seek tutoring when you do not understand. Your positive thoughts will help you to be successful.

Positive Self-Talk and Affirmations

Self-talk refers to the silent inner voice in our heads. This voice is often negative, especially when we are frustrated or trying to learn something new. Have you ever had thoughts about yourself that are similar to these:

How could you be so stupid!
That was dumb!
You idiot!

ACTIVITY

What do you say to yourself when you are angry or frustrated? Write several examples of your negative self-talk.

Negative thoughts can actually be toxic to your body. They can cause biochemical changes that can lead to depression and negatively affect the immune system.[7] Negative self-talk causes anxiety and poor performance and is damaging to self-esteem. It can also lead to a negative self-fulfilling prophecy. Positive thoughts can help us build self-esteem, become confident in our abilities, and achieve our goals. These positive thoughts are called affirmations.

If we make the world with our thoughts, it is important to become aware of the thoughts about ourselves that are continuously running through our heads. Are your thoughts positive or negative? Negative thoughts lead to failure. What we hear over and over again shapes our beliefs. If you say over and over to yourself such things as, "I am stupid," "I am ugly," or "I am fat," you will start to believe these things and act in a way that supports your beliefs. Positive thoughts help to build success. If you say to yourself, "I'm a good person," "I'm doing my best," or "I'm doing fine," you will begin to believe these things about yourself and act in a way that supports these beliefs. Here are some guidelines for increasing your positive self-talk and making affirmations:

1. Monitor your thoughts about yourself and become aware of them. Are they positive or negative?

2. When you notice a negative thought about yourself, imagine creating a new video with a positive message.

3. Start the positive message with "I" and use the present tense. Using an "I" statement shows you are in charge. Using the present tense shows you are ready for action now.

4. Focus on the positive. Think about what you want to achieve and what you can do rather than what you do not want to do. For example, instead of saying, "I will not eat junk food," say, "I will eat a healthy diet."

5. Make your affirmation stronger by adding an emotion to it.

6. Form a mental picture of what it is that you want to achieve. See yourself doing it successfully.

7. You may need to say the positive thoughts over and over again until you believe them and they become a habit. You can also write them down and put them in a place where you will see them often.

> "The most common way people give up their power is by thinking they don't have any."
> Alice Walker

Here are some examples of negative self-talk and contrasting positive affirmations:

Negative: I'm always broke.

Affirmation: I feel really good when I manage my finances. See yourself taking steps to manage finances. For example, a budget or savings plan.

Negative: I'm too fat. It just runs in the family.

Affirmation: I feel good about myself when I exercise and eat a healthy diet. See yourself exercising and eating a healthy diet.

Negative: I can't do this. I must be stupid.

Affirmation: I can do this. I am capable. I feel a sense of accomplishment when I accomplish something challenging. See yourself making your best attempt and taking the first step to accomplish the project.

ACTIVITY

Select one example of negative self-talk that you wrote earlier. Use the examples above to turn your negative message into a positive one and write it here.

REFLECTION

Write five positive statements about your future.

© Sergey Nivens/Shutterstock.com

Visualize Your Success

Visualization is a powerful tool for using your brain to improve memory, deal with stress, and think positively. Coaches and athletes study sports psychology to learn how to use visualization along with physical practice to improve athletic performance. College students can use the same techniques to enhance college success.

If you are familiar with sports or are an athlete, you can probably think of times when your coach asked you to use visualization to improve your performance. In baseball, the coach reminds players to keep their eye on the ball and visualize hitting it. In swimming, the coach asks swimmers to visualize reaching their arms out to touch the edge of the pool at the end of the race. Pole-vaulters visualize clearing the pole and sometimes even go through the motions before making the jump. Using imagery lets you practice for future events and pre-experience achieving your goals. Athletes imagine winning the race or completing the perfect jump in figure skating. In this way they prepare mentally and physically and develop confidence in their abilities. It still takes practice to excel.

Just as the athlete visualizes and then performs, the college student can do the same. It is said that we create all things twice. First we make a mental picture, and then we create the physical reality by taking action. For example, if we are building a house, first we get the idea; then we begin to design the house we want. We start with a blueprint and then build the house. The blueprint determines what kind of house we construct. The same thing happens in any project we undertake. First we have a mental picture, and then we complete the project. Visualize what you would like to accomplish in your life as if you were creating a blueprint. Then take the steps to accomplish what you want.

As a college student, you might visualize yourself in your graduation robe walking across the stage to receive your diploma. You might visualize yourself in the exam room confidently taking the exam. You might see yourself on the job enjoying your future career. You can make a mental picture of what you would like your life to be and then work toward accomplishing your goal.

> "The future first exists in imagination, then planning, then reality."
> R.A. Wilson

Successful Beliefs

Stephen Covey's book *The 7 Habits of Highly Effective People* has been described as one of the most influential books of the 20th century.[8] In 2004, he released a new book called *The 8th Habit: From Effectiveness to Greatness.*[9] These habits are based on beliefs that lead to success.

1. **Be proactive.** Being proactive means accepting responsibility for your life. Covey uses the word "response-ability" for the ability to choose responses. The quality of your life is based on the decisions and responses that you make. Proactive people make things happen through responsibility and initiative. They do not blame circumstances or conditions for their behavior.

2. **Begin with the end in mind.** Know what is important and what you wish to accomplish in your life. To be able to do this, you will need to know your values and goals in life. You will need a clear vision of what you want your life to be and where you are headed.

3. **Put first things first.** Once you have established your goals and vision for the future, you will need to manage yourself to do what is important first. Set priorities so that you can accomplish the tasks that are important to you.

4. **Think win-win.** In human interactions, seek solutions that benefit everyone. Focus on cooperation rather than competition. If everyone feels good about the decision, there is cooperation and harmony. If one person wins and the other loses, the loser becomes angry and resentful and sabotages the outcome.

5. **First seek to understand, then to be understood.** Too often in our personal communications, we try to talk first and listen later. Often we don't really listen: we

use this time to think of our reply. It is best to listen and understand before speaking. Effective communication is one of the most important skills in life.

6. **Synergize.** A simple definition of synergy is that the whole is greater than the sum of its parts. If people can cooperate and have good communication, they can work together as a team to accomplish more than each individual could do separately. Synergy is also part of the creative process.

7. **Sharpen the saw.** Covey shares the story of a man who was trying to cut down a tree with a dull saw. As he struggled to cut the tree, someone suggested that he stop and sharpen the saw. The man said that he did not have time to sharpen the saw, so he continued to struggle. Covey suggests that we need to take time to stop and sharpen the saw. We need to stop working and invest some time in ourselves by staying healthy physically, mentally, spiritually, and socially. We need to take time for self-renewal.

8. **Find your voice, and inspire others to find theirs.** Believe that you can make a positive difference in the world and inspire others to do the same. Covey says that leaders "deal with people in a way that will communicate to them their worth and potential so clearly that they will come to see it in themselves." Accomplishing this ideal begins with developing one's own voice or "unique personal significance."[10]

> ### Successful Beliefs
>
> - Be proactive
> - Begin with the end in mind
> - Put first things first
> - Think win-win
> - First seek to understand, then to be understood
> - Synergize
> - Sharpen the saw
> - Find your voice, and inspire others to find theirs

REFLECTION

List five beliefs that will help you to be successful in the future.

QUIZ

Positive Thinking

Test what you have learned by selecting the correct answers to the following questions.

1. The self-fulfilling prophecy refers to

   a. the power of belief in determining your future.
   b. good fortune in the future.
   c. being able to foretell the future.

2. Positive self-talk results in

   a. lower self-esteem.
   b. overconfidence.
   c. higher self-esteem.

3. The statement "We create all things twice" refers to

   a. doing the task twice to make sure it is done right.
   b. creating and refining.
   c. first making a mental picture and then taking action.

4. A win-win solution means

   a. winning at any cost.
   b. seeking a solution that benefits everyone.
   c. focusing on competition.

5. The statement by Stephen Covey, "Sharpen the saw," refers to

   a. proper tool maintenance.
   b. studying hard to sharpen thinking skills.
   c. investing time to maintain physical and mental health.

Create Your Future

We are responsible for what happens in our lives. We make decisions and choices that create the future. Our behavior leads to success or failure. Too often we believe that we are victims of circumstance. When looking at our lives, we often look for others to blame for how our life is going:

- My grandparents did it to me. I inherited these genes.
- My parents did it to me. My childhood experiences shaped who I am.
- My teacher did it to me. He gave me a poor grade.
- My boss did it to me. She gave me a poor evaluation.
- The government did it to me. All my money goes to taxes.
- Society did it to me. I have no opportunity.

These factors are powerful influences in our lives, but we are still left with choices. Concentration camp survivor Viktor Frankl wrote a book, Man's Search for Meaning, in which he describes his experiences and how he survived his ordeal. His parents, brother, and wife died in the camps. He suffered starvation and torture. Through all of his sufferings and imprisonment, he still maintained that he was a free man because he could make choices.

> We who lived in concentration camps can remember the men who walked through the huts comforting others, giving away their last piece of bread. They may have been few in number, but they offer sufficient proof that everything can be taken from a man but one thing: the last of the human freedoms—to choose one's attitude in any given set of circumstances, to choose one's own way. . . . Fundamentally, therefore, any man can, even under such circumstances, decide what shall become of him—mentally and spiritually. He may retain his human dignity even in a concentration camp.[3]

Viktor Frankl could not choose his circumstances at that time, but he did choose his attitude. He decided how he would respond to the situation. He realized that he still had the freedom to make choices. He used his memory and imagination to exercise his freedom. When times were the most difficult, he would imagine that he was in the classroom lecturing to his students about psychology.

He eventually did get out of the concentration camp and became a famous psychiatrist.

Hopefully none of you will ever have to experience the circumstances faced by Viktor Frankl, but we all face challenging situations. It is empowering to think that our behavior is more a function of our decisions rather than our circumstances. It is not productive to look around and find someone to blame for your problems. Psychologist Abraham Maslow says that instead of blaming we should see how we can make the best of the situation.

One can spend a lifetime assigning blame, finding a cause, "out there" for all the troubles that exist. Contrast this with the responsible attitude of confronting the situation, bad or good, and instead of asking, "What caused the trouble? Who was to blame?", asking, "How can I handle the present situation to make the best of it?"[4]

Author Stephen Covey suggests that we look at the word responsibility as "response-ability."[5] It is the ability to choose responses and make decisions about the future. When you are dealing with a problem, it is useful to ask yourself what decisions you made that led to the problem. How did you create the situation? If you created the problem, you can create a solution.

At times, you may ask, "How did I create this?", and find that the answer is that you did not create the situation. We certainly do not create earthquakes or hurricanes, for example. But we do create or at least contribute to many of the things that happen to us. Even if you did not create your circumstances, you can create your reaction to the situation. In the case of an earthquake, you can decide to panic or find the best course of action at the moment.

Stephen Covey believes that we can use our resourcefulness and initiative in dealing with most problems. When his children were growing up and they asked him how to solve a certain problem, he would say, "Use your R and I!". He meant resourcefulness and initiative. He notes that adults can use this R and I to get a good job.

But the people who end up with the good jobs are the proactive ones who are solutions to problems, not problems themselves, who seize the initiative to do whatever is necessary, consistent with correct principles, to get the job done.[6]

Use your resourcefulness and initiative to create the future that you want.

How can you create the future you want for yourself?

JOURNAL ENTRIES

Exploring Your Multiple Intelligences

Go to http://www.collegesuccess1.com/JournalEntries.htm for Word files of the Journal Entries.

Success over the Internet

Visit the College Success Website at http://www.collegesuccess1.com/

The *College Success Website* is continually updated with new topics and links to the material presented in this chapter. Topics include

- Multiple intelligences
- Emotional intelligence
- Goal setting

Contact your instructor if you have any problems in accessing the *College Success Website..*

NOTES

NOTES